S0-GGO-035

The NEGRO POTENTIAL

The NEGRO POTENTIAL

By ELI GINZBERG

assisted by

JAMES K. ANDERSON

DOUGLAS W. BRAY

ROBERT W. SMUTS

COLUMBIA UNIVERSITY PRESS

New York and London

0763048 072891

COPYRIGHT © 1956 COLUMBIA UNIVERSITY PRESS, NEW YORK

Columbia Paperback Edition 1963
Fifth printing and second paperback printing 1965

MANUFACTURED IN THE UNITED STATES OF AMERICA

CONSERVATION
OF HUMAN RESOURCES

The Conservation of Human Resources Project was established at Columbia University by General Eisenhower in 1950. It is a cooperative research undertaking involving the University, the business community, foundations, trade unions, and the Federal government. In the fall of 1955 President Grayson Kirk assigned administrative responsibility for the Project to Dr. John A. Krout, Vice President and Provost of the University. Eli Ginzberg, Professor of Economics in the Graduate School of Business, is the director of the Project.

SPONSORING ORGANIZATIONS

AMERICAN CAN COMPANY
BIGELOW-SANFORD CARPET COMPANY
CITIES SERVICE COMPANY
CLUETT, PEABODY AND COMPANY
COLUMBIA BROADCASTING SYSTEM
CONSOLIDATED EDISON COMPANY OF NEW YORK
CONTINENTAL CAN COMPANY
E. I. DU PONT DE NEMOURS AND COMPANY
GENERAL DYNAMICS CORPORATION
GENERAL ELECTRIC COMPANY
GENERAL FOODS CORPORATION
RADIO CORPORATION OF AMERICA
STANDARD OIL COMPANY (NEW JERSEY)
THE COCA COLA COMPANY
THE NEW YORK COMMUNITY TRUST

In addition to the foregoing, the Ford Foundation has also contributed toward the financing of the Conservation of Human Resources.

STAFF

DIRECTOR

Eli Ginzberg, Ph.D.

ADVISOR

Howard McC. Snyder, Major General, M.C., U. S. Army

CONSULTANT

Sol W. Ginsburg, M.D., *Psychiatry*

RESEARCH ASSOCIATES

James K. Anderson, A.B., *Manpower and Personnel*
Douglas W. Bray, Ph.D., *Social Psychology* [a]
Henry David, Ph.D., *Labor History*
John L. Herma, Ph.D., *Psychology*
Dale L. Hiestand, M.A., *Economics* [b]
John B. Miner, Ph.D., *Industrial Psychology*
Robert W. Smuts, M.A., *Economic History*

RESEARCH ASSISTANT

Bernard Roshco, M.S., *Journalism* [b]

ADMINISTRATIVE

Bryna Ball, *Administrative Officer* [b]
Reva Feldman, *Secretary*
Edith Garshman, *Secretary* [b]
Judith Nadelmann, *Statistical Assistant*
Gloria Tofano, *Secretary* [b]
Jeanne Tomblen, *Secretary to the Director*

[a] Until December 31, 1955.
[b] National Manpower Council Staff.

FOREWORD

From the start of the Conservation of Human Resources Project at Columbia University in 1950, its research plan has provided for studies of two crucial groups in the population. Individuals with unusual endowment and the capacity for superior performance have been one center of interest. The Project has also been concerned with individuals at the opposite extreme, whose handicaps of one type or another have made it difficult for them to meet prevailing performance standards. The first major publication of the Conservation Project, *The Uneducated*,[1] was the result of a comprehensive investigation of the still large number of illiterate and poorly educated persons in the United States. The problems presented by these people had been brought to the attention of the nation by the screening of the population for military service during World War II. That study sought to discover why many American citizens reached adulthood without acquiring even minimum control over the basic skills of reading, writing, and arithmetic.

It was found that the problems were more regional than national. Most of the illiterate and poorly educated persons had been born and brought up in the Southeastern states, particularly in the rural areas which until recently were more or less isolated. It was also found that illiteracy rates varied greatly among different racial and ethnic groups in the United States. The records of World War II revealed that the highest illiteracy rate was found among the Navaho Indians, who continued to speak their native tongue and had very little opportunity to attend school. A very high rate was also found among the Mexican-Americans, many of whom were migratory farm laborers. During a large part of the school year, whole families were following the ripening crops from the Rio Grande to the Canadian border. By all odds, however, the largest percent of illiterates was found among the rural Negro population of the Southeastern states.

Because of its large-scale study of the uneducated, the staff of the Conservation Project has been asked from time to time to assist in the analysis and evaluation of related materials. Two years ago the National Scholarship Service and Fund for Negro Students requested the assistance of the staff in analyzing information it had accumulated about Negro students in the South who were in the top 10 percent of their high school graduating class and had taken tests prepared by the Educational Testing Service as part of the NSSFNS's efforts to encourage capable Negro students from the South to seek admission to accredited interracial colleges. The analysis of these materials was incorporated as an addendum in an *Interim Report* of the NSSFNS in 1954.[2] Use has been made of it in preparing the chapter entitled "The Educational Preparation of the Negro."

While the Conservation Project was engaged in the study of illiteracy, the director was serving as consultant to the Secretary of the Army on manpower and personnel problems. During this period—1951-52—the Department of the Army moved energetically to integrate Negro troops fully with white troops. The chapter on "The Negro Soldier" is based partly on his observations in a series of specific assignments related to the more effective utilization of Negro manpower during the Korean conflict, as well as on earlier personnel assignments dating back to the beginning of World War II. It is impossible for any individual to see the whole of such a complex problem in an institution as large as the Army. The analysis that has been ventured has been heavily conditioned by the director's knowledge and experience and does not in any way reflect the opinions of the Department of the Army.

Early in 1955 the National Urban League, under a special grant from the Rockefeller Brothers, invited a group of consultants to reappraise the League's program for the benefit of its board of directors. As "Consultant on Training and the Use of Manpower," the director prepared a paper on the relations between the level of training and occupational achievement of Negroes. In this connection, extensive use was made of two prior studies in which the staff of the Conservation Project participated: *Occupational Choice: An Approach to a General Theory*,[3] and the 1954 report of the National Manpower Council, *A Policy for Skilled Manpower*.[4] The chapter in this book on "Better Preparation for Work" has drawn heavily on the working paper prepared for the National Urban League under the title, "Better Preparation for Better Jobs."

Since Negroes account for one fourth of the population of the South and one tenth of that of the nation, the study of their economic enfranchisement is important on its own terms. However, the subject has even greater significance. The United States is currently engaged, and will doubtless long be engaged, in assisting the less industrialized countries of the world to strengthen their economic and social structures. A deeper understanding of the economic emancipation of the American Negro—as well as of the barriers that still remain—should provide important lessons applicable to all countries where large groups still await the dawn of a day when they can develop and make better use of their potentialities.

ELI GINZBERG, *Director*
Conservation of Human Resources

Columbia University
March, 1956

ACKNOWLEDGMENTS

A number of organizations and individuals assisted in the preparation of this book by making statistical and other information available and through critical evaluation of the manuscript. The U. S. Department of Labor and the National Urban League provided background information with respect to Chapter II, "Expanding Economic Opportunities," and Chapter V, "Better Preparation for Work." The National Scholarship Service and Fund for Negro Students collected the data on the college plans of seniors from segregated high schools used in Chapter III, "The Educational Preparation of the Negro." In the original analysis of this material, the staff was aided by Richard L. Plaut, Executive Vice President of the NSSFNS.

The Department of the Army, especially the offices of the Assistant Secretary of the Army (Manpower and Reserve Forces), the Deputy Chief of Staff for Personnel, the Adjutant General, and the Surgeon General, assisted materially in the preparation of Chapter IV, "The Negro Soldier." In this connection the following individuals were particularly helpful:

Roy Davenport, Office of the Adjutant General

Lt. Colonel Steve Davis, Office of the Deputy Chief of Staff, Personnel

Eugene L. Hamilton, Office of the Surgeon General

Bernard D. Karpinos, Office of the Surgeon General

Colonel Alfred Martin, Office of the Assistant Secretary of the Army (Manpower and Reserve Forces)

Hugh M. Milton, II, Assistant Secretary of the Army (Manpower and Reserve Forces)

Colonel Josef A. Prall, Office of the Assistant Secretary of the Army (Manpower and Reserve Forces)

The manuscript was read in its entirety by and many helpful suggestions were received from:

Alvin C. Eurich, Fund for the Advancement of Education

James C. Evans, Office of the Assistant Secretary of Defense (Manpower and Personnel)

Earl D. Johnson, General Dynamics Corporation, formerly Under Secretary of the Army

James P. Mitchell, Secretary of Labor

Ann Tanneyhill, National Urban League

Major General Howard McC. Snyder, Advisor to the Project, and Dr. Henry David, Research Associate of the Project and Executive Director of the National Manpower Council, provided important guidance on many crucial points in the treatment of the material. Judith Nadelmann prepared the statistical materials for publication. Ruth S. Ginzberg assisted in the editorial revision. Jeanne Tomblen, Secretary to the Director, typed the successive drafts of the manuscript.

CONTENTS

I. THE CHALLENGE OF NEGRO POTENTIAL   3

The Progress of the Negro in America   3

Challenges for the Future   6

II. EXPANDING ECONOMIC OPPORTUNITIES   11

Opportunity and Potential   11

Negroes in the Rural South   14

Negroes in Southern Cities   19

Negroes in the North and West   29

Guides for Action   40

III. THE EDUCATIONAL PREPARATION
OF THE NEGRO   42

The Problem of Negro Education   42

Basic Education   44

High School and College   46

The Education of Negro Girls   48

*The Potential Number of High School and
College Graduates*   50

The Quality of Negro Education   53

0763048
072891

IV. THE NEGRO SOLDIER   61

  The Negro Soldier in the Past   62

  The Mental Ability of the Negro Soldier   65

  Venereal Disease   68

  Emotional and Behavior Problems   70

  The Negro Soldier in Combat   72

  Stereotypes and Reality   78

  Factors Affecting Negro Performance   81

  The Effects of Integration   86

  V. BETTER PREPARATION FOR WORK   92

  The Problem of Developing Potential   93

  The Influence of the Family   97

  The Home and the School   100

  The Armed Forces and Skill Development   102

  Preparation for Skilled Work   104

  Preparation for the Professions   108

  *The Negro Community and the Development of
  Negro Potential*   111

VI. LESSONS FOR MANPOWER POLICY   116

  Strategy for Developing Potential   116

  Future Trends: The Economy   119

  Future Trends: The Schools   124

  Future Trends: The Federal Government   127

  Future Trends: The Community   131

  Lessons for Manpower Policy   134

NOTES   139

TABLES

1. Distribution of Negro Population, by Region and Urban-Rural Residence, 1900-1950   15

2. Median Money Income of U. S. Families, by Race, Region, and Residence, 1954   16

3. The Urbanization of the South, 1900-1950   20

4. Occupational Distribution of Employed Males, by Race and Region, 1940 and 1950   23

5. Occupational Distribution of Employed Females, by Race and Region, 1940 and 1950   28

6. Occupational Distribution of Males in Nonfarm Employment, by Race and Region, 1950   31

7. Basic Literacy among Two Generations of Negro Men in the South, 1950   45

8. Elementary Schooling of Men Born in 1931-32, by Race and Region, 1950   46

9. Percent of Males Who Were High School Graduates, by Race, Region, and Age Group, 1950   47

10. College Education of Young Men, by Race and Region, 1950   48

11. Education of Young Negroes, by Sex and Region, 1950   49

12. College Education of Young Women, by Race and Region, 1950 50

13. Estimated Annual Number of Negro Male High School and College Graduates 52

14. Estimated Annual Number of Negro Male and Female High School and College Graduates 54

15. Percent Distribution among Mental Groups of Men Examined for Military Service, December 1951 103

Note: All tables based on data published by U. S. Bureau of the Census, except where otherwise noted at foot of table.

The NEGRO POTENTIAL

I: THE CHALLENGE OF
NEGRO POTENTIAL

It is no accident that the greatest progress in human freedom has taken place in the United States, a country characterized more than any other by a relative shortage of manpower throughout most of its history. The Western world has moved a fair distance from the unhappy state described by Malthus in which the number of people is kept in balance with limited food supplies by war and catastrophe. In countries where there is a surplus of population, freedom for all has often been slow in coming.

THE PROGRESS OF THE NEGRO IN AMERICA

In the United States the balance between natural and human resources has been more favorable; men have been in short supply. Wages have been consistently higher and economic opportunities consistently greater in this country than in almost any other. The Negro, of course, could not share these advantages until after the Civil War. Even then, his new legal rights were often ignored, and it was not until decades later that he began to enjoy the economic fruits of freedom. Except for a few reformers, the North had little interest in the Negro, and in the South it was simply assumed that he would remain in a subordinate role.

The disruption brought by the Civil War slowed the growth of the Southern economy for decades. The South had a surplus of every kind of manpower, including Negro manpower. Under these circumstances there was little opportunity for the Negro to buttress his new freedom with economic gains. Increasing immigration from Europe during the latter part of the century made it difficult for Negroes to gain an economic foothold in the North or West. Expanding industry preferred the skilled and even the unskilled European worker to the former slave. When new service occupations and office employment began to grow rapidly, employers preferred white female labor.

It was not until World War I that the Negro's economic opportunities improved substantially. The decline of immigration from Europe coincided with an increased demand for manpower by the armed services and expanding war industries. A large number of Southern Negroes migrated to the border and Northern states and found employment. Although many lost these jobs during the sharp depression of 1920-21, most of them were able to reestablish themselves and even to improve their positions during the prosperous twenties. Once migration from South to North began, it quickly gained momentum. No longer did hundreds of thousands of white immigrants arrive annually to provide the labor supply for our expanding urban economy. In their place came migrants from the farms, especially from the farms of the South, white and Negro alike. The first half of the thirties were bad years for white and Negro, male and female, old and young. Although conditions began to improve by the middle of the decade, the number of unemployed white workers, many of them skilled, remained so high that the Negro could find employment in only the poorest jobs.

The most spectacular economic gains for the Negro have come in the last fifteen years. The beginning of mobilization in 1940 set off an economic expansion which, for all practical purposes, has been uninterrupted from that day to this. Many sectors of industry developed an almost insatiable demand for manpower at the same time that the armed services were building up during World War II to their maximum strength of over 12 million men. Since the war, the civilian economy has continued to boom. The total number employed rose from about 47 million in 1940 to about 64 million in 1955. During the same period, the number of Negroes in nonfarm civilian employment increased from about 3 million to about 5.5 million, a proportionately larger expansion than for the labor force as a whole.

In addition to the increase in the availability of nonfarm jobs, Negro workers made equally important gains by virtue of new opportunities to obtain preferred jobs in the urban economy, and through substantial increases in the wages offered for unskilled and semi-skilled workers. As a result of the last decade and a half of sustained economic expansion, the Negro has made truly spectacular gains in the civilian economy, both in the North and South, and in the armed forces.

This is illustrated by the testimony of a senior naval officer in the spring of 1954. At a regional conference on the problem of skill called by the National Manpower Council, he reported that at the Charleston Naval Shipyard there was no longer any discrimination whatever against the Negro. Young Negroes who passed the qualifying examinations were hired as apprentices and studied and were trained side-by-side with white apprentices. When trained, they were assigned to work together with white men. All facilities on the post were used in common. The officer added that he had served in Portsmouth, N.H., in New York City, and in San Francisco, and that during the course of his working day he was unaware of being in the South. Charleston, of course, is a city steeped in Southern tradition and is in a state that has long assumed leadership in defense of white supremacy.[1]

Of course conditions in government installations are not typical of the South. Yet the response which this testimony elicited from Southern employers at the conference suggests that the near future may bring rapid improvements in the economic opportunities of the Negro throughout the region. When these employers heard the story of the success of integration at the Charleston Naval Shipyard, at Army and Air Force bases in the South, and in Tennessee Valley Authority installations, they did not respond by attacking the Federal government for interfering with states' rights. They realized that segregation on the job is bound to disappear, but they pointed out that it was impossible for Southern employers to take the lead. It was their opinion that the Federal government, by acting to eliminate segregation in employment within its orbit of responsibility, could help the South by leading the way toward a solution of this difficult problem.

CHALLENGES FOR THE FUTURE

The American society has many unique characteristics, and one is the ability of its people to adjust to rapid change. The progress of the American Negro during the past fifteen years has been possible only because of the striking capacity that individuals and institutions have shown to adopt new ways of thinking and behaving. Although progress has been remarkable, racial discrimination in employment still exists. The major concern of this monograph is to analyze the problems that must be solved before the Negro can take full advantage of his new and rapidly growing opportunities resulting from the steady reduction of discrimination in employment. Overt job discrimination is only one of the important hurdles which must be overcome before color can disappear as a determining factor in the lives and fortunes of men.

The concept of potential that provides the focus for this book requires some elaboration. Several decades ago social scientists assumed that the performance of adults was largely determined by innate qualities. Later they stressed the importance of the environment in determining adult behavior. More recently a broader approach has gained ascendency. The prevailing view among social scientists holds that there are no significant differences among groups as to the distribution of innate aptitudes, or at most very slight differences. On the other hand, differences among individuals are very substantial. The extent to which an individual is able to develop his aptitudes will largely depend upon the circumstances present in the family within which he grows up and the opportunities which he encouters at school and in the larger community.[2]

We know from psychology that the early years of an individual's life exercise a major influence on his later development. We know from history and the social sciences that deeply ingrained practices affecting large groups can be altered only slowly. The past lives on even as changes occur, and changes are not absorbed automatically or easily. The discrimination so long practiced against the Negro has been so pervasive that relatively few Negroes are now able to take full advantage of their new opportunities. Even now, almost a century after the Civil War, the civil and legal rights of the Negro are not always respected, particularly in the rural South. If the Negro is to be able to take immediate advantage of the new economic opportunities that are becoming open to him, it is important to understand the nature of the barriers that remain and the actions required to remove them.

The next chapter, "Expanding Economic Opportunities," provides a summary account of the very substantial progress that the Negro has been able to make during the past decade and a half as a result of the expansion of the economy. The opening up of new opportunities for employment both in the urban South and in other parts of the country has set the stage for striking gains in the development of Negro potential. Not only have many Negroes been able to find work more nearly consonant with their abilities, but the higher incomes that most Negroes have been able to earn enable them to provide their children with a better start in life.

During the last fifty years the Negro has made spectacular gains on the educational front. A census study in 1947 revealed that while one third of all Negroes above the age of sixty-five were unable to read or write, only 4 percent in the age group fourteen to twenty-four were illiterate.[3] At the same time, however, the educational level of the white population has also risen greatly. Economic integration of the Negro means that for the first time he will have to compete directly with the white majority. Chapter III, "The Educational Preparation of the Negro," sets out the serious deficiencies in the quantity and quality of the education of Negroes compared to the education of the white population, not only in the South but in all parts of the country. If economic integration is to succeed, special efforts must be made to reduce as rapidly as possible, and eventually to eliminate, the differences between white and Negro education.

Chapter IV, "The Negro Soldier," points up the difficulties of objectively assessing the performance of any disadvantaged group. Appraisal of the facts is based inevitably upon the prior experience and preconceptions of the individuals who pass judgment. The Negroes who saw service during World War II were more handicapped, on the average, by their civilian background and experience than were white soldiers. But their performance was also significantly affected by the prevailing pattern of segregation. The chapter also reviews the impact on the utilization of Negro manpower of the change from segregation to integration that took place primarily during the period of Korean hostilities. It shows how, with determined leadership, significant changes can be introduced in a relatively short time.

Chapter V, "Better Preparation for Work," focuses on the changes required within the Negro community before its members will be in a position to take full advantage of their new economic opportunities. The willingness of employers to hire properly qualified Negroes is one necessary condition. But, before the number of highly qualified Negroes can be increased substantially, it is also necessary that young Negroes acquire through their home, family, and community environments, the new attitudes, habits, and values which will enable them to derive the full benefits of better school instruction.

The last chapter, "Lessons for Manpower Policy," seeks to identify the major factors responsible for the remarkable gains of the Negro minority since the beginning of World War II. Few countries in the world are completely free of the evil of discrimination. The lessons learned about the economic enfranchisement of the American Negro should prove useful wherever men of intelligence and good will seek to remove the restrictions which hamper disadvantaged groups. Only when the potential with which men and women are born is allowed to develop fully can a society have both a sound foundation for economic progress and individual contentment.

II: EXPANDING ECONOMIC
OPPORTUNITIES

During the last twenty-five years, both American society and the position of the Negro within it have changed fundamentally. It is therefore difficult to view in proper perspective the present status, the unsolved problems, and the future prospects of the American Negro. Within the short span of a quarter century the nation has experienced a blistering depression, World War II, the challenge of Communism, conflict in the Far East, the longest and most sustained period of industrial expansion in its entire history, and major retreats and striking advances in the area of civil liberties. The transformation of the status of the Negro during this same period is largely the result of these major events.

OPPORTUNITY AND POTENTIAL

The present position of the Negro in American society is far better than any he has known in the past — better, indeed, than his most optimistic friends could have predicted fifteen years ago. But it would be an error to look only backwards and to see only the gains. The next chapter will illuminate how far the education of Negroes still lags behind the education of whites. Likewise, despite the striking gains of the Negro on the economic front, particularly since 1940, he does not yet share fully in the opportunities our economy presents.[1]

In a culture such as America's, it is difficult to overstress the importance of economic opportunity, for so much of the total life of a citizen and his family depends upon the income he earns. It is important, therefore, to explore not only the extent of the opportunities now open to Negroes to rise on the occupational scale and to improve their economic position, but also to review carefully the obstacles which continue to make it difficult or impossible for Negroes to take advantage of new opportunities. The key to the unlocking of potential is always found in the first instance in the widening of opportunity. But the successful development of potential and its effective utilization after it is developed require much more than this. Our industrial society is becoming daily more demanding about the types of manpower it requires, particularly when the worker has responsibility for the operation and maintenance of expensive capital equipment. If the color barrier could be eliminated overnight, that fact alone would not materially improve the position of the Negro. Just as white men now must compete with each other in terms of aptitude, education, and skill, so too does this same challenge face the Negro as the artificial employment barriers which stand in his way are successively eliminated.

The exploitation of opportunity, therefore, must wait upon the development of ability. But, conversely, the development of specialized abilities must wait upon opportunity. As long as the Negro community recognized that there was no possibility of one of its members obtaining employment as an engineer, neither Negro educational institutions nor Negro parents could sensibly encourage the younger generation to go through the long and arduous program of engineering training. Before 1950, few Negro engineers were being trained. But with the strong and persistent demands of American industry for engineering and related technical personnel after the outbreak of hostilities in Korea, a growing number of engineering jobs were opened to Negroes. Since then, a considerable number of Negro students have been willing to make the investment required to prepare for engineering careers.

The development of Negro potential depends on the expansion of economic opportunity in a still deeper sense. For the Negro population to be able to compete on an equal basis for professional, scientific, managerial, skilled, and other desirable jobs will require a revolution in all levels of Negro education, and beyond this, in the values and aspirations, the living conditions, and the community environments of large groups in the Negro population. All of this, in turn, depends in large part on the opportunities of Negroes to earn larger incomes. Thus, the opening up of engineering jobs to qualified Negroes in the North has no immediate meaning for the Negro farm hand in Alabama. Nor will it have meaning for his children or grandchildren unless he is first able to escape the poverty, ignorance, and isolation of the marginal farm in the South. But if he does escape, even if only to a job as a sweeper in a factory, his children's opportunities to develop their potential will be much enhanced.

This chapter considers the economic progress of the Negro population in the recent past, the present circumstances of Negroes, and the major challenges yet to be faced. The past, the present, and the probable future are significantly different for different groups of Negroes in various parts of the country. Three major groups have been distinguished for separate consideration: Negroes in the rural South, Negroes in Southern cities, and Negroes in cities elsewhere in the country.

NEGROES IN THE RURAL SOUTH

The 1950 Census reported a total Negro population of about 15 million. As Table 1 shows, slightly over one third were then living in the rural South, one third in the urban South, and slightly less than one third in cities outside of the South. At the turn of the century, 90 percent of all Negroes lived in the South, and three fourths were in the rural South. In the whole country, at that time, less than one fourth of the Negroes lived in cities, compared to about two fifths of the whites. By 1950, as the result of a steady migration into cities, and especially into Northern cities, over three fifths of the Negroes were urban residents, almost exactly the same proportion as among the white population. The size of migration from the rural South is indicated by the fact that in 1950 there were 2.6 million Negroes who had been born in the South but were living in other regions. These migrants constituted one fifth of all living Negroes born in the South and half of all Negroes then living outside of the South. Seven of the sixteen Southern states actually had fewer Negroes in 1950 than in 1940 although the total Negro population had increased by over 2 million during the decade.

The living conditions of most of those who remain in the rural South are extremely poor. A recent analysis by the Department of Agriculture, based on 1950 Census data, found only 20 percent of the Negro farm population in medium- or high-income farm areas whereas almost 60 percent of the white farm population lived in such areas. Forty percent of the Negro farm population lived

TABLE 1. DISTRIBUTION OF NEGRO POPULATION BY REGION AND
URBAN-RURAL RESIDENCE, 1900-1950 [a]

	1900	1920	1940	1950 [b]
South [c]	90%	85%	77%	68%
Rural	74	64	49	35
Urban	16	21	28	33
Other Regions	10%	15%	23%	32%
Rural	3	2	2	2
Urban	7	13	21	30
Total Rural	77%	66%	51%	37%
Total Urban	23%	34%	49%	63%

[a] All tables based on data published by U. S. Bureau of the Census, except where otherwise noted.
[b] Because of a change in the Census definition of urban between 1940 and 1950, these figures are not exactly comparable with earlier data.
[c] Alabama, Arkansas, Delaware, Florida, Georgia, Kentucky, Louisiana, Maryland, Mississippi, North Carolina, Oklahoma, South Carolina, Tennessee, Texas, Virginia, Washington, D. C., West Virginia.

in seriously low income areas.[2] The results of this concentration of rural Negroes in the poorest farming areas are illustrated by Table 2 which shows that the median money income in 1954 of Negro farm families in the South was $742. Money income, of course, does not measure the full consuming power of farm families. However, the relative position of Negro farm families is indicated by the fact that they had only half as much money as white farm families in the South, and only one third as much as white farm families in the whole country.

Although most Negro farm families are having a hard struggle even to maintain what can only be described as a marginal existence, they have a very high birth rate. In the total rural farm population of the United States in 1950, there were 518 children under five years of age to every thousand women aged fifteen to forty-nine. Among

TABLE 2. MEDIAN MONEY INCOME OF U. S. FAMILIES, BY RACE, REGION, AND RESIDENCE, 1954

	White	*Nonwhite* [a]	*Percent Nonwhite of White*
Total U. S.	$4,339	$2,410	56
Total Urban	4,827	2,876	60
South	4,428	2,425	56
Northeast	4,837	3,243	67
North Central	5,059	3,283	65
West	4,812	n.a.	n.a.
Total Rural-Farm	2,157	763	49
South	1,516	742	49

[a] Data are given here and elsewhere for all nonwhites together whenever such data are available from Census publications and separate Negro data are not available. Since Negroes constituté 95 percent of the nonwhite population, data for nonwhites represent a close approximation of data for Negroes alone.

n.a.: not available.

Negro farm families, the ratio was almost 700 children per thousand women.[3] The Department of Agriculture has estimated that unless migration from the farms continues, the number of young people reaching working age on farms in many areas in the South will be twice as great as the number who are likely to stop working because of death or old age.[4] Unless the already exceedingly low standard of living is to be depressed still further, there are only two possible alternatives to continued large-scale migration. Agriculture must be further improved or more industry established.

The productivity of Southern agriculture has been increasing substantially because of improved methods, larger investments in capital and fertilizer, larger farm units, and a shift from cotton and tobacco to diversified farming and cattle raising. But, as the staff of the Rural Life Coun-

cil of the Tuskegee Institute has shown, most Negro farmers have not benefited from these important developments.
With limited education, with little or no capital of their
own, and without ready access to credit, Negro and poor
white farmers have been left behind as Southern agriculture has moved ahead. Nor has the Negro gained from the
development of large, scientific, commercial farms, since
they have provided steady, reasonably well-paid employment to very few Negroes.

Even if some Negroes do manage to improve their farms
to the point where they provide a good living, the need for
large-scale migration would not be eliminated. Southern
agriculture has far too many workers already. Increasing
farm productivity is certain to lead to a still greater decline
in the number of farmers and farm workers. Under these
circumstances the most disadvantaged families will find
it increasingly difficult to maintain even a precarious toe-
hold in the agricultural economy.

A second possibility is a more rapid increase in the number of industrial plants located in the heart of the poor
farming areas. Most Southern states are actively seeking
to attract new industries and the Federal government is
becoming increasingly concerned with the problems of
the depressed agricultural areas of the country, particularly in the South. But even if there is a substantial increase in industrial employment in these poor farming
areas, it is doubtful that it will materially help the farm
Negro for a long time. As will be seen, the Negro has
been able to obtain few jobs in Southern industry, and the
odds will remain against him where there are large numbers of poor white farmers awaiting opportunities for industrial employment.

New industrial plants in the South rarely have difficulty

in recruiting for routine jobs the necessary number of white workers from surrounding areas. One large aircraft factory in the deep South has employees who commute from over thirty different counties. Recently, an executive of a southern railroad stated that "you can drive a stake almost anywhere along the eastern Seaboard in the South . . . and in most of those areas, farming communities, you can build a mill where you drive the stake and get from 500 to 2,000 workers from that area without having to build a single house." [5] The basic reason for this is illustrated by Table 2, which shows that although white farm families in the South earn considerably more than Negro farm families, their incomes are much lower than those of farm families elsewhere, and only about one third of the earnings of urban whites in the South. As long as there remains a large surplus of white workers in the South, employers will have little incentive to challenge tradition by hiring Negroes for more industrial jobs.

There are many reasons for concern over what has been happening to the Negro farmer over the last two or three decades. Although it is true that the worst exploitation which formerly typified tenancy and sharecropper status has been eliminated, Negroes have not participated proportionately in the large increase in the number of farmers who own the farms they operate. Southern agriculture is no longer easy to enter, for it frequently requires capital of from $15,000 to $20,000. Dairy farming has developed rapidly in recent years, but it is frequently necessary for the tenant dairy farmer to invest more funds of his own than most Negroes have or are able to secure. The rapid industrialization of Southern farming places new hurdles in the path of the unskilled Negro agricultural laborer, for agriculture now requires many skills. It is not surprising that Lewis W. Jones concluded, in his study of the Negro farmer, that, "Negro farmers as a group have lost ground in the period 1920-50 by any criteria used." [6]

In the future, as in the past, large numbers of young Negroes who grow up on marginal farms will seek a livelihood in the cities of the South or elsewhere. From the viewpoint of preparation for work these Negroes will long remain severely handicapped. They come from the parts of the South where race prejudice runs deepest, where Negroes are most frequently deprived of their legal rights, where the struggle against school integration is most intense and will be most prolonged. Beyond the general handicaps of this environment are the specific handicaps that grow out of poverty, ignorance, and isolation. Young Negroes from depressed farm areas will continue to grow up with only the most elementary agricultural skills. Unless there is a much more radical improvement in the schools of these areas than seems likely, the young Negro and, to only slightly lesser degree, the young white will be poorly prepared to meet the minimum demands of industry and of urban society at large in terms of the ability to read, write, and compute. He will have little basis for adjusting to the demands of an industrial and commercial community which stresses self-reliance, work discipline, and planning for the future. And, of course, he will have none of the specific skills that are useful in urban employment. In all of these respects and in many more, the young farm Negro will remain ill-equipped for the life which will face him when he seeks a job in a city.

NEGROES IN SOUTHERN CITIES

One of the outstanding economic developments during the last generation has been the urbanization and industrialization of the South. Table 3 shows that since the turn of the century urbanization has been much more rapid in the South than in the United States as a whole. As late as 1920 only one fourth of the Southern population lived in urban centers, compared to half of the total population of the country. By 1950, nearly half of all Southerners were urban residents, compared to less than two thirds of the total population of the country. Between 1920 and 1950 the Negro population in the urban South increased from about 2.3 million to almost 5 million. It is easy, especially for Northerners, to think of the Negro as either the Negro on a Southern farm or the Negro migrant in a Northern city. Almost one third of the Negro population of the country, however, lives in the cities of the South.[7]

TABLE 3. THE URBANIZATION OF THE SOUTH, 1900-1950

	Percentage of Population in Urban Residence		Percentage of Southern Urban Population
Year	U.S.	South	Which Was Negro
1900	40	15	41
1920	51	25	30
1940	57	35	28
1950 *	64	47	25

* Because of a change in the Census definition of urban, these data are not exactly comparable with earlier data.

Although the growth of the Negro population in the urban South has been spectacular, the urban white population has grown even more rapidly. Consequently, while there have been large increases in the number of Negroes living in Southern cities since 1900, the ratio of Negroes to whites in Southern cities has fallen steadily. In 1900, Negroes accounted for over 40 percent of the inhabitants

of Southern cities. By 1950, they represented only 25 percent. Eventually, this growing predominance of whites
may contribute to a reduction of racial tensions. Mean-
while, however, the urban Negro must compete for jobs
against a constantly growing number of whites.

As we have seen, the rural Negro comes to the city ill-
prepared to meet its challenges. Once there, he usually
has difficulty in adjusting to urban life. He probably has
trouble finding a job, and he certainly has trouble locating
decent housing. Yet the migration of Negroes from Southern farms to Southern cities has been a voluntary movement; it reflects the belief that, however difficult conditions are in the city, they are better than on the farm.
That there is basis for this belief is illustrated in Table 2,
which shows that the urban Negro family in the South
earns more than three times as much money as the Negro
farm family. It is important to note also that the Negro
feels greater personal security in the more disciplined
metropolitan centers of the South than in the countryside,
where passions can be more easily inflamed and group
action directed against him.

The economic position of the Negro in Southern cities
can be appraised by considering three factors—whether
he can get a job, what kind of job he gets, and whether
he has a chance for promotion. Between 1940 and 1950,
nonagricultural employment in the South expanded by
almost 60 percent for white women, almost 40 percent for
white men, 30 percent for Negro men, and only 7 percent
for Negro women. These figures emphasize that whites are
becoming an increasingly larger majority of the urban
labor force in the South. Yet these data should not be taken
as a measure of the relative opportunities of the two races
to obtain nonfarm employment. One reason for the fact

072891

that far more whites than Negroes entered urban employment within the South during this period is that the total Negro labor force in the region was not expanding as rapidly as the total white labor force. There were, in turn, two reasons for this situation. As we have seen, many Negroes were moving North. Second, a smaller proportion of the Negro population was working in 1950 than in 1940. Negro boys and girls were staying in school longer, old people were retiring sooner, and relatively fewer Negro women were working. All of these developments, of course, reflect improvements in the economic circumstances of Negro families.

The Negroes who remained at work in the South did find increasing opportunities for nonfarm employment between 1940 and 1950. Indeed, Tables 4 and 5 show that, relative to the number of workers of each race, the shift from farm to nonfarm employment in the South was somewhat greater for Negroes than for whites. In 1940, Negro men in the South were divided evenly between farm and nonfarm employment. By 1950, there were almost twice as many in nonfarm work as in farm work.

Significant gains were made in many occupational areas, even at the top levels. Although there are still very few Negro men working as professionals, managers, officials, or proprietors, substantial percentage increases were registered in these fields, mainly as a result of the growing size and prosperity of the Negro communities in Southern cities. This development has fostered the growth of medical care, education, retailing, insurance, and other services for Negroes. In these fields, segregation operates in reverse, for almost all jobs in Negro enterprises serving Negro customers are reserved for Negroes. A visit to the Negro suburbs of Atlanta or Birmingham provides visible

TABLE 4. OCCUPATIONAL DISTRIBUTION OF EMPLOYED MALES, BY RACE AND REGION, 1940 AND 1950

	1950				1940			
	SOUTH		OTHER REGIONS		SOUTH		OTHER REGIONS	
	Negro	*White*	*Negro*	*White*	*Negro*	*White*	*Negro*	*White*
Professional, technical, and kindred workers	2.0%	7.0%	2.6%	8.3%	1.6%	4.9%	3.1%	6.3%
Managers, officials, and proprietors	1.4	11.5	3.0	11.7	.9	10.2	2.8	10.9
Clerical and sales workers	2.4	12.9	7.8	14.2	1.2	11.7	5.6	14.8
Craftsmen, foremen, and kindred workers	6.4	18.5	10.8	20.4	3.6	12.8	7.7	16.7
Operatives and kindred workers	18.6	18.7	27.4	20.8	10.9	16.0	19.6	20.0
Service workers	11.2	3.7	21.4	5.8	11.2	4.5	32.6	6.6
Nonfarm laborers	23.6	5.8	24.9	7.0	20.6	6.1	24.5	8.1
Total nonfarm workers	65.6	78.1	97.9	88.2	50.0	66.2	95.9	83.4
Farmers and farm workers	34.4	21.9	2.1	11.8	50.0	33.8	4.1	16.6
Total	100.0	100.0	100.0	100.0	100.0	100.0	100.0	100.0

evidence of the fact that a considerable number of Negroes have managed to reach the upper income levels. In clerical and sales work, the situation is much the same. There are still very few Negro men in these occupations. Nevertheless, there have been large percentage gains in recent years resulting largely from the expansion of Negro enterprises.

At the skilled worker level, the circumstances are different. Skilled Negroes have always been an important part of the construction industry in the South, and, recently, they have been accepted as automobile mechanics. In these fields, Negroes have been able to profit from the growing size and prosperity of the whole of the urban South, not just from the development of the Negro community. Because both construction and automobile industries have been flourishing for years, many more Negro men have found employment in these fields.

In spite of these gains at the upper occupational levels, the major increases in nonfarm employment of Negro men in the South have been at the lower levels, particularly in employment as operatives. Even these increases, however, represent progress. Any kind of steady urban employment, even as a laborer, provides an income well above that of the average Negro farmer or farm worker. The man who leaves a poor farm may never advance beyond a job as laborer himself, but as long as he works in the city he can provide his family with a better living, and his children will grow up with knowledge of city ways and with far better schooling than they could obtain in the country.

Although employment opportunities for Negro men in Southern cities have improved substantially since 1940, they are still severely restricted. Table 4 shows that only one out of eight Negro men in the South was employed in a white collar or skilled nonagricultural job in 1950, compared to one of every two white men. Within each of the major occupational groups, moreover, opportunities for a significant number of Negroes were limited to a few specific kinds of work. Thus, two thirds of the professional men were clergymen or teachers in Negro institutions. There were less than 500 Negro engineers in the whole South, compared to well over 100,000 white engineers. Few Negro men held salaried positions as managers or officials. Most of those classified as managers, officials, or proprietors were the owners of small businesses. Almost half of them owned retail stores, bars, or restaurants.

In manufacturing, Negro men have obtained jobs mainly as laborers, truck drivers, or janitors. Except in establishments where the work is heavy, dirty, hot, or otherwise disagreeable, such as foundries or sawmills, there are few Negroes in any kind of production jobs. In 1950, for instance, there were over 10,000 white men working as operatives in the Southern automobile industry, but fewer than 350 Negro men. In general, the production line jobs from which Negroes are barred provide better pay and lighter work than the jobs for which Negroes are hired. More important is the fact that experience on the production line is the major route to skilled and supervisory jobs in manufacturing.[8]

The largest increases in nonfarm employment of Negro men in the South in recent years have been among those working as operatives. Three fourths of the Negro operatives in 1950 were concentrated in nine groups of occupations. The largest group, drivers of trucks, busses, taxis, etc., accounted for one third of the total. The other large groups worked in lumber mills, mines, laundries, food processing plants (one of the most seasonal of all industries), parking lots and garages, chemical factories, metal refineries and foundries, and power plants.

Negro operatives, in short, were concentrated in the least desirable occupations. Moreover, Negro men working as operatives in the South were outnumbered almost two to one by men still lower down in the occupational hierarchy — service workers, more than half of whom were janitors or porters, and unskilled laborers in all sectors of the urban economy.

Even in the South, however, there is a small but growing number of places where segregation in employment is not practiced and where men are hired, trained, assigned, and promoted without regard to their color. In spite of the tendency of the Federal government to follow prevailing local practices, it has been easier for Negroes to obtain better jobs in the Federal installations that are scattered throughout the South, than in private industry. And with each year their opportunities in the Federal Civil Service will probably increase as the Federal government makes an increasing effort to put nondiscriminatory policies into effect. On the periphery of the South a considerable number of employers have abandoned segregated employment practices and have opened significant new opportunities for Negro workers. Examples can be found in Florida, North Carolina, Tennessee, and Texas, and there are even some integrated plants in the heart of the deep South. Where integration has succeeded, employers have usually had the full backing of union leadership, if not of union members. Generally, integrated plants are branches of Northern companies.

These advances are important because they represent a beginning of integration and a demonstration that it is possible, but they have not yet affected more than a minute fraction of the Negroes in Southern cities. During the last decade or two an increasing number of Negro men have been able to find work in the expanding urban economy of the South. But the great majority of them have been employed at the bottom of the job ladder and have no chance of moving up. These circumstances are the result of community pressures and union practices as well as of employer prejudices. The white members who control Southern unions have generally been reluctant to give up their monopoly of the better jobs.

Female employment has been expanding more rapidly than male employment in Southern cities. Nevertheless, the employment opportunities of Negro women in the South have been even more severely restricted than those of men. Table 5 shows that there was some shift from farm to nonfarm employment between 1940 and 1950. The improvement of Negro education has provided more teaching jobs for Negro women. As was true of men, the growth of Negro enterprises has led to a substantial percentage increase in employment in the clerical and sales fields, but the number of women in these fields is still very small. The proportion of Negro women working as operatives almost doubled between 1940 and 1950, but these occupations still accounted for only one tenth of all Negro working women. Moreover, more than half of the operatives worked in laundries. The small number of Negro women in manufacturing was concentrated in the poorest jobs in the food processing, tobacco, garment, and a few other industries.

In spite of their gains in various other sectors of the urban economy, 64 percent of all Negro women employed in the South in 1950 were still in the service occupations, almost as high a proportion as in 1940. The major change,

Table 5. Occupational Distribution of Employed Females, by Race and Region, 1940 and 1950

| | 1950 | | | | 1940 | | | |
| | SOUTH | | OTHER REGIONS | | SOUTH | | OTHER REGIONS | |
	Negro	*White*	*Negro*	*White*	*Negro*	*White*	*Negro*	*White*
Professional, technical, and kindred workers	6.3%	14.0%	4.6%	13.3%	4.4%	15.8%	3.7%	14.6%
Managers, officials, and proprietors	1.3	5.6	1.4	4.6	.6	5.1	1.1	4.2
Clerical and sales workers	3.5	41.0	9.0	40.7	.9	31.5	3.0	33.6
Craftsmen, foremen, and kindred workers	.4	1.4	1.1	1.7	.1	.8	.3	1.2
Operatives and kindred workers	9.5	19.7	24.7	20.3	5.0	21.4	10.6	20.4
Service workers, private household	45.4	3.0	35.8	4.4	58.8	7.9	64.4	11.9
Other service workers	18.2	10.7	20.9	11.7	8.9	10.5	15.9	11.9
Nonfarm Laborers	1.2	.6	2.1	.8	.9	.8	.8	.9
Total and farm workers	85.8	96.0	99.6	97.5	79.6	93.8	99.8	98.7
Farmers and farm workers	14.2	4.0	.4	2.5	20.4	6.2	.2	1.3
Total	100.0	100.0	100.0	100.0	100.0	100.0	100.0	100.0

as Table 5 indicates, was a shift from private household work to employment in other service jobs. Over one third of the Negro women in nonhousehold service employment in 1950 worked as waitresses, cooks, counter girls, and in other jobs in eating and drinking places.

If the Negro in the urban South is not to be permanently confined to the least skilled jobs which pay the lowest wages, Southern industry must be willing to hire Negroes, not only for a limited number of menial positions from which they cannot rise, but also for the broad range of semi-skilled positions from which a man can, with application and seniority, rise into the skilled and supervisory ranks. Unless and until this takes place, the Negro will remain on the lower rungs of the economic ladder in the urban South.

As far as the Negro woman in the South is concerned, it is clear that she cannot soon anticipate access to new opportunities which would lead to responsible, well-paid jobs. Such opportunities are severely limited even for white women in all parts of the country. The major help for the Negro woman would be the abandonment of the prevailing attitude that she is suited only for service work. Not until Negro women are able to obtain clerical and sales work and semi-skilled factory work will it be possible for even a few of them to climb to skilled, supervisory, or managerial positions.

NEGROES IN THE NORTH AND WEST

It is clearly a gross oversimplification to consider the employment opportunities of all Negroes outside of the South as a single problem. Negroes have quite different positions in the economies of different Northern cities. On the other hand, almost all Negroes outside of the South are

3763048

urban residents, and most of them live in the larger cities. Moreover, the economic role of the Negro in the Northern city is different enough from his role in the South to justify contrasting the two.

Between 1940 and 1950, when the Negro population as a whole increased by 17 percent, the population of Negroes in the North increased by 52 percent and in the West by 234 percent, while there was only a 3 percent increase in the South. In New York City the nonwhite population increased from under 500,000 to over 750,000; in Chicago from under 300,000 to over 500,000; in Detroit, from 150,000 to over 300,000. On the West Coast, the rate of increase was even larger. In Los Angeles, the nonwhite population increased from 100,000 to 211,000; in San Francisco and Oakland from 46,000 to 136,000.

Outside of the South, very few Negroes work on farms. This is the most striking contrast between the two regions. Table 6 shows that there is not a great deal of difference in the occupational distribution of Negro men in nonfarm employment in the South and the rest of the country. The percentages of Negro men who are managers, officials, proprietors, or skilled workers are only slightly higher in Northern cities. The Negro's chances of becoming a professional are slightly less in the North than in the South. The most conspicuous advantage of the Northern Negro man is that he has greater opportunity to obtain clerical or sales work. About the same proportion of nonfarm workers in the two areas are operatives. The proportion at the bottom of the occupational ladder—laborers and service workers—is only slightly smaller in the North. The occupational opportunities of Negro men are much more narrowly restricted than those of white men in all parts of the country. Among male nonfarm workers in 1950, slightly less than one fifth of the Negroes in the South, slightly less than one fourth of the Negroes outside the South, but over three fifths of the whites were employed in nonmanual occupations or in skilled jobs.

TABLE 6. OCCUPATIONAL DISTRIBUTION OF MALES IN NONFARM EMPLOYMENT, BY RACE AND REGION, 1950

	SOUTH		OTHER REGIONS	
	Negro	White	Negro	White
Professional, technical, and kindred workers	3.0%	8.9%	2.7%	9.4%
Managers, officials, and properties	2.2	14.8	3.1	13.3
Craftsmen, foremen, and kindred workers	3.8	16.5	8.0	16.1
Clerical, sales, and kindred workers	9.7	23.8	11.0	23.1
Operatives and kindred workers	28.3	23.9	27.9	23.6
Service workers	17.1	4.7	21.8	6.6
Laborers	35.9	7.4	25.5	7.9
	100.00	100.0	100.0	100.0

Why, then, have so many more Negroes gone to Northern cities than Southern cities in recent years? Wherein are the Negro's opportunities greater in the North than in the South? There are a number of answers to these questions. In the first place, it has undoubtedly been easier for the Negro to find work in the Northern city. Unable to draw so easily upon the enormous reserve of underemployed white farm labor which characterizes the South, Northern employers have been more pressed to meet their needs for unskilled and semi-skilled workers during the last fifteen years of economic expansion and high employment. Faced with a larger need, and, in most instances, less influenced by prejudice against the Negro, Northern and Western employers have been more willing than those in the South to turn to the Negro population as a new labor supply.

Closely related to these circumstances is the fact that the wages paid for unskilled and semi-skilled work — the type of work most Negroes perform — are higher in the North than in the South. Consequently, even though about the same proportions are employed in unskilled and semi-skilled jobs in the South and elsewhere, the earnings of urban Negroes have been much higher in the North. Table 2 shows that in 1954 urban Negro families in the Northeast and the North Central regions had about one third more income than those in the South.

There is at least one other reason for the fact that Negroes are more attracted to the cities of the North and West. In spite of widespread prejudice, discrimination, and *de facto* segregation, cities outside the South are not committed to a pervasive and rigid system of segregation. Without minimizing the importance of other aspects of this difference, it must be emphasized that it has a profound effect on the pattern of job opportunities.

While the proportion of Negro men who reach the upper occupational levels is only slightly higher in the North, the Negroes in upper-level jobs in the North have found their opportunities in a much wider range of activities. Thus, as we have seen, two thirds of the Negro professional men in the South in 1950 were teachers in Negro schools or clergymen in Negro churches. Less than one fourth of the Negro professional men in the Northeast, however, were clergymen or teachers. The rest worked in a wide variety of professional occupations. Similarly, almost half of the Negro managers, officials, or proprietors in the South were owners of retail establishments. This was true of only about one fifth in the Northeast, where opportunities for salaried managerial work were somewhat greater.

Thus, both within the South and elsewhere, the Negro who aspires to professional, managerial, or entrepreneurial status is faced by advantages and handicaps specific to the area. In the South he is rigidly confined to the Negro community, but that community is large, and within it he is protected from competition from whites. In the North, he lacks some of the special opportunities provided by a large and rigidly segregated Negro community, but he has evened the scales by making his way somewhat further in the larger community. The same generalizations apply to clerical and sales work.

In skilled work, too, the Negro is able to enter a wider variety of occupations in the North. Half of the Negro men working as craftsmen, foremen, and kindred workers in the South in 1950 were carpenters, masons, painters, plasterers, or plumbers. In the Northeast, these occupations accounted for only one-fourth of the Negro men in skilled or supervisory work. Indeed, the old-line, highly organized building trades are often the ones in which the Negro has the most difficulty obtaining employment in the North. On the other hand, his opportunities to obtain skilled work in manufacturing are somewhat better than in the South.

Between 1940 and 1950, as Table 4 indicates, the opportunities for upper-level employment for the urban Negro in the North barely kept even with the huge growth of the Negro population. There was a slight increase in the proportion employed in clerical and sales work, and a somewhat larger gain in the proportion in skilled and supervisory work. The major change, however, was a large shift from service work to the operative occupations.

Almost all of the operative occupations which included large numbers of Negroes in the South in 1950 were also among the leading occupations in the North. Again, however, Negroes outside the South were not so severely limited as to the range of occupations. It has been noted that nearly three fourths of the male Negro operatives in the South were employed in nine groups of occupations distinguished by low pay, irregularity of work, unpleasant working conditions, or by the fact that they are essentially "dead-end" jobs. In the Northeast these same occupational groups accounted for about 55 percent of the Negro operatives. In addition, substantial numbers of male Negro operatives in the Northeast worked in garment factories, paper, textile, and yarn mills, and in various branches of the fabricated metal products industries, including machinery manufacturing.

In the North more Negroes have been accepted in semi-skilled jobs which may lead to skilled or supervisory work. In the automobile industry, for example, promotion is most usually the result of experience and seniority. In the South, as we have seen, Negro men accounted for only about 3 percent of all men working as operatives in the automobile industry. In the North Central states, where they were a much smaller proportion of the labor force, Negroes, many of them fresh from the South, accounted for almost one tenth of the operatives in this industry.

Since 1940, as Table 5 indicates, the urban Negro woman outside the South has made greater occupational progress than the Negro man. Moreover, in terms of occupational opportunity, she has a considerably greater advantage over the Negro woman in the South than is true in the case of the Negro man. In 1950, among Negro women employed in the North and West, the proportion in clerical and sales work was three times as high as in 1940, and more than double the proportion in the South in 1950. The proportion working as operatives was more than double both the 1940 ratio and the proportion in the South in 1950. At the beginning of that decade, nearly two thirds of the Negro women working in Northern cities were servants in private households. By 1950, only slightly more than one third were domestic servants.

Nevertheless, in the North as in the South, and in 1950 as in 1940, the outstanding fact about the Negro women working in cities is that most of them were service workers —servants, cleaning women, waitresses, hospital attendants, cooks, etc. Although they have made great advances in clerical and sales work since 1940, less than one out of ten had such jobs in the North in 1950, compared to two out of five white women.

In order to evaluate the occupational progress of the Negro in the North we must consider briefly his circumstances before World War II and the factors which stimulated the changes which have taken place since then. Although the North has never been committed to a formal, legal system of segregation, neither was it committed to the principle of equality of opportunity for Negroes before the war. Negroes were excluded from many unions and from many apprenticeship programs. As in the South, moreover, it was difficult for them to obtain the unskilled and semi-skilled production jobs which normally constitute the first step toward skilled work. High unemployment throughout most of the 1930's meant that the Negro was in a very poor position to press his claims. Since large numbers of white men were out of work, many of whom were better trained and had more experience, the Negro found it harder than ever to obtain employment.

World War II brought striking changes. First, the surplus labor market disappeared almost overnight and in place of too many workers there were suddenly too few. In place of intermittent work or no work at all, which had been the lot of many during the 1930's, Negroes now found jobs waiting for them—jobs which provided not only a full week's work, but often considerable overtime in addition. A further result was the employment of large numbers of Negroes in industries where they had never worked before. Another significant factor was the new fair employment practices policy enforced in many sectors by the Federal government, which made it illegal for employers to discriminate against individuals on the basis of race or religion. Similar policies have since been enacted into law by fifteen states and by some local governments.[9]

The labor shortages of World War II were not the only reason for break-throughs in the job market. Considerable weight must also be given to the increasing awareness of many white citizens, including leaders in industry and the trade unions, that discrimination against the Negro was a violation of basic American tenets and should be eliminated as rapidly as possible. For many years, the National Urban League had been pursuing a carefully balanced program of analysis, persuasion, and training to help sympathetic white employers to adjust to the transition from an all-white to a mixed labor force. The League's continuing efforts met with increasing success under the more favorable conditions of the war and postwar periods. Concerted pressure from interested community groups was especially effective in opening sales positions to Negro women. Many employers who had argued that they could not hire Negroes because of consumer resistance found that they could no longer afford to be prejudiced and therefore began to place Negro women on the sales floor.

One of the most important gains made by the Northern Negro in the last fifteen years came about as a result of the growth of trade unionism and the Negro's acceptance in industrial unions. Under the contracts of most industrial unions, both job security and eligibility for training and promotion are heavily dependent on seniority. For the Negro union member, these provisions constitute an important protection against discrimination. There are still a few unions that refuse to admit Negroes. There are others where the bylaws have been altered to eliminate discrimination, but where the Negro has little chance of acceptance. Nevertheless, the last fifteen years brought a major change in the policies of most of the important unions throughout the United States outside of the South and, to some extent, even in the South.

In spite of these developments, as we have seen, the proportion of Northern Negroes in the upper-level occupations did not increase appreciably between 1940 and 1950. In evaluating this fact, however, it is important to recall that the cities of the North and West succeeded in absorbing almost 2 million new Negro residents during the decade. Since many of the new inhabitants were poorly educated migrants from the South, the surprising fact is that the proportion of Negroes in upper level jobs did not decline. The actual number of Negro men outside the South in the upper level jobs—that is, all occupations excepting operatives, service workers, and laborers — increased from less than 110,000 in 1940 to almost 270,000 in 1950. In 1940 there was a substantial supply of Negro high school and college graduates available for these jobs.

As a result of the preceding decade of unemployment, re-inforced by racial discrimination, most of them were working in jobs which made little use of their abilities and education.

A recent analysis of 1950 Census data on the relation between education and income among the white and Negro population shows that the well-educated Negro has improved his position considerably since 1940. But it also shows that Negroes still earn far less than whites who have the same amount of education. In the North and West as well as the South, Negro college graduates earned less in 1949 than whites who had attended but not gradu-ated from high school. In 1940 Negro college graduates earned less than whites who had not graduated from gram-mar school. Both in the South and in other regions, the dif-ference between Negro and white earnings tends to be greater, the more education individuals have acquired.[10]

The urban South also succeeded in absorbing a large increase in its Negro population and, at the same time, in placing a growing proportion of Negro workers in upper-level jobs. The important difference between the regions in this respect is that in the South the advance-ment of Negroes has been tied very closely to the develop-ment of the Negro community and to the level of employ-ment in a few skilled trades where Negroes have been widely accepted. In the North, substantial numbers of Negroes have been able to secure employment in a wider variety of industries and activities at all occupational levels in the community at large. While the great majority of Northern Negroes are still in unskilled and semi-skilled jobs, growing numbers are in jobs which normally con-stitute one of the early steps towards skilled, supervisory, or managerial work.

This does not mean, however, that Negroes will automatically be promoted to better-paying and more responsible jobs. Few workers can acquire sufficient skill to warrant promotion without some training, either in a formal program or informally from supervisors or fellow workers. Even after the skills are acquired, the worker must still be selected for promotion. This is what one interested employer has called the "challenge of injecting Negroes into positions of higher skills." In discussing the problem at a recent conference, he stressed the importance of training both before and after entrance upon the job. As we will see, the lower educational level of Negroes represents a serious handicap when they compete with whites for the better jobs in an organization. But there is no question that much remains to be done within industry before qualified Negroes have equal access to industrial training and to skilled and supervisory positions.

It is at the management level, however, that the least progress has been made. It is difficult to assess how near we in the United States are to the time when important companies will be willing to recruit young Negro college graduates as executive trainees in the same way that they have long been recruiting white graduates. The first important step in this direction is the growing willingness of large companies to hire Negroes for scientific and technical work. In these fields the qualified Negro graduate now has a chance to compete with the white graduate. In fact, because the demand for scientific and technical personnel is so great, almost every qualified Negro can get a good job, if not always the job of his preference. This breakthrough is still limited to the field of technical staff work, but if the trend continues, as it most likely will, a few of these staff people will undoubtedly begin to move over into "line" management just as white engineers and scientists frequently do.

Within the short span of fifteen years, the economic opportunities of the Negro in the United States have vastly increased. Yet, complacency is unwarranted, for even in the cities of the North and West the Negro is far from having equality of opportunity. To reach this goal he needs much help. No matter how rapid the migration from Southern farms continues to be, the birth rate there is so high that large numbers of Negroes will undoubtedly continue to till the soil for several generations. Like their white neighbors who farm under similar conditions, most of them are struggling against tremendous odds. They need better education, better health services, more agricultural extension work, easier credit. Above all else, they need a broadening of their economic base through the establishment of industrial units which could provide them not only with an alternative to farm employment but also with the added income that is necessary to break through the old circle of ignorance, poverty, and underemployment. Nothing short of a major concerted effort on the part of the Federal government, together with state and local governments, and reinforced by various types of voluntary effort, will introduce a sufficient number of dynamic factors to make a significant impact upon these handicapped regions. To develop solutions is a major challenge to the country, not to the depressed areas of the South alone.

The immediate challenge in the urban South is to increase the kinds of jobs available to Negroes. Their position in Southern industry today is not too different from what it was in many sectors of the North twenty and thirty years ago. The immediate and primary need is for Negroes to be hired as production workers so that they will have the opportunity to acquire the experience and training necessary before they can move into the skilled occupations. At present most jobs available to them in Southern industry lead nowhere.

Equally pressing is the need for a break-through for Negro women beyond the narrow confines of service work. If they are to make any significant gains in the near future, they must be accepted in factories as well as in clerical and sales employment. Although, as we will see, the education of the Negro in the South is inadequate, many Southern Negroes are high school or college graduates. Their primary need is for employment opportunities outside of the Negro community.

In the regions outside of the South there are also several challenges. A large number of employers still refuse to hire Negroes. This is particularly true in the major fields of female employment, many of which have only recently been opened to Negro girls and women. Furthermore, even in the North, the majority of Negroes are still concentrated in jobs which are not likely to lead to advancement. These are serious problems, but progress toward solving them is already substantial. The greatest needs that remain are that industry be willing to train able Negroes, to promote them to skilled and supervisory positions, and, above all, to consider them for management positions.

III: THE EDUCATIONAL
PREPARATION
OF THE NEGRO

Because of deficiencies in their home and community environments and in the schools they attend, Negroes have far less opportunity to acquire a solid education than do most of the white population among whom they live. A man's education is exceedingly important in determining his eventual position on the economic scale. Except for sports, the arts, and a few other fields, most preferred occupations require a college degree. A recent study of the National Manpower Council, *A Policy for Skilled Manpower*, shows that employers throughout the country are increasingly reluctant to hire people who are not high school graduates. A high school diploma is more and more a prerequisite for any young person to be considered for various types of industrial training which would enable him to move out of an unskilled or semi-skilled job into a skilled or supervisory position.[1]

THE PROBLEM OF NEGRO EDUCATION

An evaluation of the education of Negroes is, therefore, essential to an understanding of his changing role in the American economy. Consideration cannot be limited to secondary and higher education. As we will see, there are still many Negroes who had so little or such poor education that, for all practical purposes, they are illiterate. A man without a high school education is handicapped, but an illiterate man is almost crippled; he can obtain only the most menial, dead-end jobs in the urban economy. In *The Uneducated* it was reported that industry in both the South and North is refusing to hire illiterates. Likewise, the armed forces believe that when men are available for only twenty-four months' service it is far too costly to accept those who cannot read or write.[2]

There is another reason to consider the elementary as well as the secondary and higher education of Negroes. The number of Negroes able to complete college successfully depends on the number who graduate from high school well-prepared for college work. Likewise, the number who are able to complete high school depends upon the number who receive adequate elementary schooling.

The following pages consider the amount of education received by Negroes from three different viewpoints. Comparison of the present with the past will show that great strides have been made, especially in the last fifty years. However, since the Negro is both seeking to compete and forced to compete with the white members of the community, it is also essential to compare his education with that of the white population. Finally, we will estimate under varying assumptions the possible increases in the number of Negroes who might complete high school and college in the future.

In most of the following comparisons, data are presented separately for the South and the rest of the country. At the turn of the century almost 90 percent of the Negro population lived in the South. Even today, about two thirds of all Negroes live in the South, and half of those living in the rest of the country were born in the South.

The educational problems of the Negro stem largely from his position in the South and from the relative backwardness of the region as a whole. Although the Southern economy has made enormous progress, especially since the beginning of World War II, the region still has less resources to support education and other public services than has the rest of the nation.[3]

The educational preparation of young people in this country is too often judged in terms of the amount of schooling they have passed through and the number of diplomas and degrees they have acquired. Since the effect rather than the amount of schooling is what counts in the end, the concluding section of this chapter assesses the quality of Negro education in both the South and the North.

BASIC EDUCATION

In the absence of current data on the number and distribution of illiterates in the population, data on the number of years of school completed serve as a rough measure of basic literacy. The armed forces have found that unless a man can read and write at least as well as the average fifth-grade student, he must be regarded as a "functional illiterate."

Table 7 shows that one out of every five Negro men reaching adulthood in the South in 1950 had not completed the fifth year of school. This represents a big improvement over the record of the preceding generation, half of whom were functional illiterates. Table 8 shows, however, that in the South functional illiteracy was still three times as frequent among young Negro men as among young white men. This means that even if discrimination in employment based solely upon color were completely eliminated, Southern industry would prefer white to Negro workers. The handicap which Negroes would face in industry because of illiteracy, even if discrimination were totally eliminated, is illustrated by the recent experience of the armed forces. Even though the military has abolished all formal distinctions based on color, the mental test for determining eligibility for service results in the rejection of a much higher percentage of Negroes than of whites.

TABLE 7. BASIC LITERACY AMONG TWO GENERATIONS OF NEGRO MEN IN THE SOUTH, 1950

	Older Generation (born 1905-09)	*Younger Generation (born 1931-32)*
No schooling	9.2%	1.7%
One to four years of schooling completed	40.0	17.7
Total with less than five years of schooling completed	49.2	19.4

Outside of the South, as Table 8 also shows, there were few functional illiterates among Negroes or whites. Studies of migrants have found that the very poorly educated are less mobile than the better educated. The low percentage of illiterates among Northern Negroes confirms the conclusion that the functionally illiterate Southern Negro generally remains in the South. The adjustment of those who do come North is handicapped by the fact that Northern employers seldom encounter illiterates and are not willing to make allowances for them. A Northern family is not likely to hire a Negro woman who is unable to take a telephone message, nor a Northern plant to take on a Negro who cannot find his own time card on the rack.

TABLE 8. ELEMENTARY SCHOOLING OF MEN BORN IN 1931-32,
BY RACE AND REGION, 1950

	SOUTH		OTHER REGIONS	
	White	*Negro*	*White*	*Negro*
Less than five years of schooling completed	6.2%	19.4%	1.7%	5.2%
Five to eight years of schooling completed	25.5	41.7	13.9	21.9
Total with no more than elementary schooling	31.7	61.1	15.6	27.1

Table 8 also shows the percentage of young adult Negro
males who, according to the 1950 Census, terminated
their formal education with graduation from elementary
school or before. In spite of striking improvements in
Negro education, three out of every five young Negro
males in the South had no high school education. The
proportion of Northern Negroes who did not attend high
school was much lower, about one out of four. Indeed, in
this respect, Northern Negroes had a better record than
Southern whites. In the North as well as the South, however, the percentage who did not go to high school was
almost twice as high for Negroes as for whites. In view of
the importance attached to high school graduation by
employers, it is evident that a high percentage of the
Negroes and a substantial part of the white population
are barred by poor educational preparation from serious
consideration for the better jobs in the community.

HIGH SCHOOL AND COLLEGE

Table 9 shows the percentages among several groups in
the population in 1950 who had at least a high school
diploma. Fewer than one third of the men who were forty

to forty-five years old in 1950 had graduated from high school, even among whites in the North. Among the younger generation, aged twenty to twenty-four, over half of the white males in the North, and over two fifths of the same group in the South were high school graduates. Although the rate of improvement among Negroes was greater, they remained far behind the white population. In the South the proportion of white boys graduating from high school was almost three times as high as the proportion of Negro boys. Outside of the South the whites had almost a two-to-one advantage. In the South only one out of seven Negro boys finished high school, and in the North, only one out of three. In the country as a whole four out of five young Negro men were not high school graduates in 1950.

TABLE 9. PERCENT OF MALES WHO WERE HIGH SCHOOL GRADUATES, BY RACE, REGION, AND AGE GROUP, 1950

	SOUTH		OTHER REGIONS	
	White	*Negro*	*White*	*Negro*
Older generation (born 1905-09)	24.1	5.4	30.4	13.5
Younger generation (born 1926-30)	42.0	14.7	56.4	31.3

The higher education of young white and Negro men is shown in Table 10. Even in the areas outside of the South only about three young Negro men out of every hundred graduate from college. Throughout the country the advantage of whites over Negroes is greater at this level than at any other level except in the achievement of basic literacy. Relatively fewer Negroes graduate from high school, and of those who do, fewer enter college. And of those who enter college, fewer graduate. The table also shows that in the South the main loss of Negroes from the educational system occurs before high school graduation. Of those who graduate from high school in the South, the proportions who enter and who complete college are almost as high for Negroes as for whites. In the North, however, one out of five white high school graduates, but only one out of nine Negro high school graduates, completes college.

TABLE 10. COLLEGE EDUCATION OF YOUNG MEN,
BY RACE AND REGION, 1950

	SOUTH		OTHER REGIONS	
	White	*Negro*	*White*	*Negro*
Graduated from high school [a]	42.0%	14.7%	56.4%	31.3%
Entered college [b]	20.3	6.2	24.2	10.1
Graduated from college [c]	8.8	2.2	10.6	3.4

[a] Among 20-24 year age group.
[b] Among 24 year age group.
[c] Among 25-29 year age group for whites, and 30-34 year age group for Negroes.

THE EDUCATION OF NEGRO GIRLS

Table 11 compares the education of Negro men and women. It shows that Negro women are ahead of men at every educational level in the South, and at each level up to college in the North. It should be noted, however, that more white girls than boys graduate from high school also.

In the South there are twice as many functional illiterates among young Negro men as among young Negro women. Considerably more Negro girls than boys begin high school. Although a larger percentage of the girls who begin high school do not graduate, the girls still have a pronounced lead over the boys at the end of high school. A higher proportion, but a smaller number, of male high school graduates begin college. The lead of the girls is again widened in college because more of those who begin remain until graduation. The number of Negro women who graduate from college in the South is more than one third larger than the number of men.

TABLE 11. EDUCATION OF YOUNG NEGROES,
BY SEX AND REGION, 1950

	SOUTH		OTHER REGIONS	
	Male	*Female*	*Female*	*Male*
Less than five years of schooling completed [a]	19.4%	9.1%	5.2%	4.0%
No more than elementary schooling [a]	61.1	45.7	27.1	21.3
At least high school graduation [b]	14.7	21.8	31.3	40.1
At least some college [c]	6.2	7.4	10.1	9.8
College graduation [d]	2.2	3.0	3.4	3.0

[a] Among 18-19 year age group.
[b] Among 20-24 year age group.
[c] Among 24 year age group.
[d] Among 30-34 year age group.

Outside of the South the differences between Negro men and women are less marked. More Negro girls than boys enter high school, and about one third more girls than boys graduate. Just as in the South, a larger percentage of the boys who do graduate from high school go on to college. In the North, however, the number of boys attending and graduating from college is slightly larger than the number of girls. The proportion of Negro girls graduating from high school is twice as high in the North as in the South. Yet, because the proportion of high school graduates who continue until they finish college is twice as high in the South, the same percent of Negro women receive college degrees in both areas.

Even though Negro women, on the whole, are better educated than Negro men, they still receive far less education than white women. Table 12 shows that in the South, the percentages completing high school, entering college, and completing college are about twice as large for white women as for Negro women. The same is true in the North, except at the level of high school graduation where the advantage of whites over Negroes is somewhat smaller. The table also indicates that about the same proportion of women attend college in the South and the rest of the country.

TABLE 12. COLLEGE EDUCATION OF YOUNG WOMEN,
BY RACE AND REGION, 1950

	SOUTH		OTHER REGIONS	
	White	*Negro*	*White*	*Negro*
Graduated from high school [a]	48.0%	21.8%	64.4%	40.1%
Entered college [b]	14.4	7.4	17.0	9.8
Graduated from college [c]	6.1	3.0	6.2	3.0

[a] Among 20-24 year age group.
[b] Among 24 year age group.
[c] Among 30-34 year age group.

During the last generation, the Negro has made great educational progress. Yet at every level from learning to read and write to graduation from college, he is still far behind the white population. This is true, in different degrees, in the North as well as the South, and for both men and women.

THE POTENTIAL NUMBER OF HIGH SCHOOL AND
COLLEGE GRADUATES

In order to appreciate the magnitude of the penalty paid by the Negro population and the nation for the

Negro's lag in education, it is not enough to consider only the proportions of Negroes completing various levels of education. It is also important to estimate how many Negroes now receive the benefits of high school and higher education, and how many more might be able to under different circumstances. This is the purpose of the rough estimates appearing in the following tables.

Table 13 presents the potential number of Negro males who might graduate annually from high school and college. It estimates first the number of high school graduates in 1950, and how many of them could be expected to graduate from college under conditions prevailing at that time. The table then shows how these figures would be changed if Southern Negroes achieved the educational level of Negroes outside the South, of whites in the South, and of whites in the North.[4]

If the education of Southern Negro males were brought up to the level of Southern white males, the actual number of high school graduates in the region would be tripled, from about 11,000 to about 32,000. If the education of Northern Negroes were brought up to that of whites in the North, the number of Negro high school graduates in the North would be nearly doubled, from almost 14,000 to almost 25,000. Thus, if the differences between the races with respect to high school graduation were eliminated within each region, there would be 32,000 high school graduates in addition to the 25,000 who actually graduated. If the educational disadvantages of the South were also eliminated—that is, if all Negroes were brought up to the level of Northern whites—then the total number of Negro graduates would be increased by another 11,000, to nearly 68,000.

Similarly, if the differences between the races with re-

Table 13. Estimated Annual Number of Negro Male High School and College Graduates

	SOUTH		OTHER REGIONS		U.S. TOTAL	
	High School Graduates	College Graduates	High School Graduates	College Graduates	High School Graduates	College Graduates
1950	11,200	2,200	13,800	1,600	25,000	3,800
If Negroes Were Raised to Educational Level of:						
Negro males in other regions	23,800	2,800	13,800	1,600	37,600	4,400
Southern white males	32,000	7,400	18,400	4,400	50,400	11,800
White males in other regions	42,800	8,400	24,800	5,000	67,600	13,400

spect to college graduation were eliminated within each region, there would be 12,400 Negro college graduates, compared to the estimated number of 3,800. If the differences between regions were also eliminated, there would be still another 1,000 graduates.

Table 14 shows that under the same assumption, the number of high school graduates, both male and female, would increase from 65,000 to 158,000. The number of college graduates would increase from 9,400 to 23,200.[5]

THE QUALITY OF NEGRO EDUCATION

So far we have considered only the quantity of education received by Negroes. But not only do Negroes complete fewer years of schooling than whites; the education they do receive is, for the most part, far inferior. The psychologists who work in the armed forces induction stations in the Southeastern region occasionally discover a graduate of a Negro high school who is unable to pass the mental examination, even though a passing score represents approximately fifth-grade achievement. While the failure of a Negro high school graduate is unusual, there is a considerable number of failures among Negroes who have completed as much as nine or ten years of school.

The Speaker of the House of Representatives of the State of Georgia has declared that "Negro education in Georgia is a disgrace. What the Negro child gets in the sixth grade, the white child gets in the third grade." [6] The president of one of the leading Negro institutions of higher learning in the South has repeatedly stated that a high proportion of the graduates of Southern Negro high schools are unable to cope with college instruction unless they are provided with from six months to a year of special

TABLE 14. ESTIMATED ANNUAL NUMBER OF NEGRO MALE AND FEMALE HIGH SCHOOL AND COLLEGE GRADUATES

	SOUTH		OTHER REGIONS		U.S. TOTAL	
	High School Graduates	*College Graduates*	*High School Graduates*	*College Graduates*	*High School Graduates*	*College Graduates*
1950	30,600	5,800	34,200	3,600	64,800	9,400
If Negroes Were Raised to Educational Level of:						
Negroes in other regions	59,600	6,200	34,200	3,600	93,800	9,800
Southern whites	74,800	13,200	42,800	7,600	117,600	20,800
Whites in other regions	100,200	14,600	57,600	8,600	157,800	23,200

additional training. As the following pages will show, there are ample data confirming these impressions.

On the average, white men screened for military service have completed about 12 years of school, compared to about 8 years for Negroes. Nearly three fourths of the white men achieve scores on the armed forces qualification test which place them in "Group III" or above, which means that they have about average or above average capacity to absorb military training. Among the Negroes, only a little over one fourth are in the highest three groups. The difference in test scores is very much greater than we might expect from the difference in years of schooling alone. It is so great that it would seem to be explicable only in terms of the poorer quality as well as the smaller quantity of schooling received by Negroes.

The same conclusion emerges from a review of recent studies of the performance of Negroes on scholastic aptitude tests. As the staff of the National Manpower Council pointed out in *A Policy for Scientific and Professional Manpower*, "Most social scientists now believe that there are no inborn differences in intellectual potential between Negroes and the rest of the population, or that such differences, if they exist, are very small. Yet, a study made a few years ago of college freshmen showed that the average freshman in a Negro college scored only a little higher on aptitude tests than the lowest-ranking freshman in the average college. This finding testifies both to the sensitivity of the test to prior educational experience and to the great differences between the educational opportunities of Negroes and whites." [7]

The most directly relevant data on the quality of Negro education in the South has been secured by the National Scholarship Service and Fund for Negro Students through a study made in connection with their scholarship program during the academic year 1953-54. The Fund's objective was to encourage more of the best Negro students from Southern high schools to apply for admission to good interracial colleges. The Fund was able to offer modest scholarships to encourage such students.[8]

The field staff of the Fund visited eighty-one segregated schools in forty-five large cities in the South and urged students who were in the upper 10 percent of the senior class and who had pursued a college preparatory course to take a test to determine whether they were qualified for admission to a good interracial college. The Educational Testing Service at Princeton prepared a modified college entrance examination and established a qualifying score. The passing grade was set considerably below the norm used on national examinations. A total of 1,485 students were tested, which accounted for approximately one third of all students in the top 10 percent of the senior classes of all accredited Negro high schools, and a higher proportion of all high-standing seniors who had taken college preparatory courses. Just about half, 737 students, qualified.

A special analysis was prepared for the Fund to determine on the basis of this sample the maximum number of Negro students who might have secured a passing score if all who were eligible had taken the examination. Instead of the 737 who did in fact qualify, the total might have been 1,200. This means that only three out of every hundred graduates from segregated Negro high schools in the South were qualified for a good interracial college. It is worth noting in passing that girls accounted for 70 percent of the entire group that was tested, since there were more girl than boy seniors and the girls more frequently pursued a college preparatory course.

The Educational Testing Service also had the scores of 6,026 candidates of all races from public high schools who took the regular college entrance examination test in May, 1953. Although the results are not competely comparable, they do provide a rough measure of the difference between the two groups. Only 6 percent of the top-ranking Negroes from Southern high schools did as well as or better than the average student who took the regular test.

Analysis of the study indicated beyond any doubt that the overwhelming majority of graduates from Southern Negro high schools cannot compete with the average graduate of the average high school. Yet, it also indicated that, within a short period, it should be possible to double the 200 annual entrants from segregated high schools to good interracial colleges. The next year actually showed a 33 percent increase. Within five years it might be possible, with proper scholarship assistance, and with expanded guidance and testing programs, to increase the number to 1,500 or even 2,000.

It is not only in the South, where segregated schools are still almost universal, that the Negro receives inferior education. Not long ago, in one Northern metropolis, the superintendent of a school district in which the great majority of students were Negroes was asked to estimate the intellectual capacity of his students at the end of the eighth grade. It was his considered judgment that less than 1 percent of the entire student body in the area had an intelligence quotient of 120 or above. This conclusion may be contrasted with the fact that in an upper middle-class white suburban community about 30 percent of the student body would have an IQ of 120 or above.

Many circumstances outside the school are responsible in some measure for this gross difference in developed mental ability. These include the low incomes of most Negro families and the adverse conditions under which most Negroes live. Nevertheless, considerable weight must be given to poor schools. Frequently these schools are segregated in fact if not in law. There are many communities outside of the South where, as a result of residential segregation, almost all Negroes attend schools in which there are few if any white students. Often these schools in predominantly Negro neighborhoods are in serious disrepair, are staffed by inexperienced teachers, and are unable to provide instruction geared to the widely different abilities of their students. A major preoccupation of the teacher in many of these schools is the maintenance of discipline. Under these circumstances there is little the school can do to counteract the multiple disadvantages of the home and community environment of the Negro child. Handicapped at home and again handicapped at school, the potential of many Negro students in Northern cities is seriously underdeveloped by the end of their elementary schooling.

Ferguson and Plaut have recently reported on a survey of the school performance of Negroes in the June, 1952 graduating classes of 32 public high schools in California, Colorado, Connecticut, Illinois, Indiana, Massachusetts, Minnesota, New Jersey, New York, Ohio, and Pennsylvania. Out of total senior class enrollment of 10,400, Negroes accounted for 3,300, or over one third. Yet, only 53 Negroes were in the highest quarter of their class. With respect to class standing the white students did fifteen times better than the Negroes. The survey also ascertained that only 24 of these 53 students had taken college preparatory courses. Thus, less than one out of every hundred Negro seniors was fully qualified for college admission.[9]

As the authors point out, there are several reasons for this very poor showing. One major difficulty is, as we have mentioned, the failure to develop potential during the first eight years of schooling. Also important is the failure to guide capable Negro students to high schools where they can obtain good academic education and to provide conditions that would motivate them to put forth their best efforts while in school.

Of crucial significance in the educational process is the quality of the teacher. In terms of formal educational qualifications, Negro teachers in many parts of the South are at least as well-prepared as white teachers. This is so, in part, because the Negro college graduate has few other professional employment opportunities. On the average, however, Negro teachers are much less able than white teachers in spite of the fact that they have about the same amount of formal preparation. Like other young Negroes, those preparing to teach are usually handicapped by poor schools and deprived backgrounds. A recent study by Arthur L. Benson of the Educational Testing Service analyzed the abilities of prospective white and Negro teachers in states with segregated schools. Test scores of white and Negro freshmen in Southern teacher-training institutions and liberal arts colleges in which a large number of the freshmen were planning to teach were compared with the test scores of freshmen in the country as a whole. The average score of the white freshmen in the Southern schools was exceeded by 65 percent of the freshmen throughout the country. The average future Negro teacher in the South ranked below 95 percent of the freshmen in the whole country.[10]

A parallel study was also made of almost 1,500 seniors in thirty-seven colleges located in nine Southern states who were preparing to teach. On a professsional information test, the white seniors in the South achieved an average score which was very near the national average, but the average Negro senior, like the Negro freshman, was bettered by 95 percent in the nation as a whole. With respect to English expression tests, the Negro seniors did somewhat better. In terms of the combined score on all phases of the testing program, white seniors in the South were again near the national average, but the Negro senior who was preparing to teach in the South was outscored by 96 percent of all college seniors. Moreover, the scores of Negro seniors who came from rural backgrounds and were planning to teach in rural areas were much lower than the scores of other Southern Negroes.

The Negro population labors under a double educational handicap. Since the Negro goes to school for fewer years than do whites, he receives far less preparation for life and work. What schooling he does receive is of inferior quality and therefore has less value than the schooling received by whites. A major weakness of Negro education is the poor preparation of Negro teachers. It has not been possible under segregation to break the cycle of poorly prepared Negro teachers teaching severely handicapped Negro students. Significant improvement will probably have to wait for progress in integration. This was surely a major concern of the Supreme Court when it handed down its epoch-making decision to end segregation in public education.

IV: THE NEGRO SOLDIER

The most spectacular increases in the opportunities of Negroes during the past generation have occurred in the armed forces. During World War II almost all Negro troops served in segregated units, but within a few years after the end of the war Negro soldiers were fully integrated. A review of the conditions which prevailed during World War II, when over 2 million Negroes were screened for military service and more than a million were called to active duty, can provide important insights into the relation between segregation and the utilization of Negro potential. In turn, a review of the factors that led to integration, and of its results, can illuminate the way in which the performance of Negroes is determined by the presence or absence of opportunities. This chapter is also concerned with showing how the characteristics that Negroes acquire in civilian life have affected their performance in the military. Finally, the rich body of information available about the characteristics and performance of the Negro soldier can be used to appraise the extent to which judgments about him were based on facts, and the extent to which they reflected the preconceptions of the white population.

The analysis which follows will concentrate on the utilization of the Negro in the Army. During World War II the Army included the Air Corps. Combined, their peak strength of 8.3 million was approximately double that of the Navy, which included the Marine Corps. Moreover, Negro strength has consistently been proportionately greater in the Army than in the Navy, partly because the Army has had to make greater use of Selective Service draftees to meet its manpower needs, and partly because it was more difficult to absorb large numbers of Negroes on a segregated basis in the Navy. A fuller and more significant story can therefore be told by studying the integration of the Negro soldier rather than of the Negro sailor.[1]

THE NEGRO SOLDIER IN THE PAST

Negroes have participated in all of our country's wars. It is estimated that about 5,000 Negroes participated in the Revolutionary War and that 3,000 saw service during the War of 1812. Much larger numbers were involved during the Civil War; it is estimated that as many as 200,000 Negroes served under arms for some period. During the Spanish-American War the Negro strength of the Army was about 10,000. During World War I over 400,000 Negroes served in the Army, and over 1,300 of these were officers.[2]

Several developments that took place during World War I had an important effect on later Army thinking about Negro manpower. The first large-scale mental testing of troops took place in 1917-18. Negroes scored very poorly on these tests. For many, this was scientific proof of the innate mental inferiority of the Negro. It was not until later that it was recognized that many white boys who had grown up under severely disadvantaged conditions, with little or no opportunity for schooling, also performed poorly on the tests. The conviction that the Negro was basically inferior to the white man was widely accepted before psychologists pointed out that Negroes who had been brought up in Northern states scored, on the average, somewhat higher than did white men from the more isolated farming areas of the South.

A second legacy from World War I was the conviction that the Negro was not a good fighting man. This conclusion was based on the performance of the 92nd Division and elements of the 93rd Division in France, in which all of the enlisted personnel and a considerable proportion of the officers were Negroes. There was evidence that the 369th Infantry Regiment, under French command, gave a satisfactory account of itself, and no less an authority than the Secretary of War, Newton D. Baker, warned against generalizing about the fighting ability of the Negro solely on the basis of the record of these two divisions. Nevertheless, Army doctrine in the postwar period was highly critical of the fighting ability of the Negro.

The third important legacy from World War I was the Army's recognition of the difficulties that would confront it in the event of any large-scale inflow of Negro manpower. The Army recognized that an increasing proportion of Negroes were living outside of the South, in areas where, despite widespread restrictions, segregation was not imbedded in law. Yet, since the South practiced strict segregation, the Army concluded that it would have to continue its own segregated pattern, and that it could not afford to engage in social experimentation in the middle of an emergency. It remembered the serious riots involving Negro troops during World War I and did not overlook the race riots in St. Louis, Chicago, and Detroit in the postwar period. The avoidance of such trouble in a future emergency became a major objective of Army planning.

The curriculum of Army schools between the two wars stressed three conclusions about the utilization of Negro troops: First, World War I had proved that a very high proportion of Negro manpower was poorly endowed mentally and would therefore present a major challenge to efficient utilization in a future mobilization. Second, the Negro, when given an opportunity to fight in World War I, had failed. Finally, if large numbers of Negroes were again mobilized, the Army would be confronted with major problems of military discipline and public relations, growing out of probable friction between Negro and white troops, as well as between Negro troops and the civilian population.

Between the World Wars the Regular Army had four authorized Negro regiments — the 9th and 10th Cavalry and the 24th and 25th Infantry. There was great pride in the Negro community concerning these four regiments and there was a constant excess of Negroes seeking to enlist in them. At the outbreak of World War II, about 3,600 Regular Army enlisted men were Negroes, about 2 percent of total Army strength. But between 1920 and 1940 only one Negro succeeded in graduating from West Point.

Had the Army been in a position to determine its mobilization plans for Negro manpower without reference to the American public and Congress, it would probably have moved along the following lines. It would have attempted to induct a much smaller percentage than Negroes formed of the population as a whole, thereby reducing the numbers of poorly educated persons in the Army. It would have taken a disproportionate number of Negroes from the North, where Negroes were better educated and had more skills. And, finally, it would have organized most, if not all, Negroes into segregated labor battalions. Actually, in World War II, Negro strength in the Army nearly reached the proportion that Negroes formed of the population. Negroes comprised just under 10 percent of the Army's enlisted strength, compared to just over 10 percent of the population. The Army was able to take a relatively higher percentage of Negroes from the North, however, and a high proportion of Negroes were assigned to and served throughout their military careers in the equivalent of segregated labor units.

Not able to cope with the problem of Negro manpower by controlling the inflow, the Army was forced throughout the war to improvise new policies for making more effective use of the very large numbers who were drafted, In doing so, it responded to the challenge from within and to the challenge from without. It had to develop, within the limits of the time and resources available, improved methods of utilizing the large numbers of poorly educated Negro personnel who had been drafted. And, under the prodding of Negro leaders, supported by the White House, it had to open new opportunities for Negroes to serve in accordance with their abilities and the training they had received. But, although the Army's personnel policies and practices were changed in various ways, the basic pattern of segregation remained.

THE MENTAL ABILITY OF THE NEGRO SOLDIER

The Negro's performance as a soldier during World War II may be evaluated in terms of many criteria. In this chapter, attention will be focused on four standards: his mental abilities, his physical condition as influenced by venereal disease, his emotional and behavior problems, and, finally, his record in combat. The available statistical data and other information will first be reviewed, and then an effort will be made to interpret the forces operating in civilian and military life that were responsible for determining the performance of Negro soldiers.

When the Army reached its peak strength of slightly less than 8.3 million early in 1945, there were just under 700,000 Negroes on active duty, of whom about 7,000 were officers. During the entire course of the war, 923,000 Negroes were called to active duty as enlisted men. Negroes, who represented 10.3 percent of the males of military age in the country, accounted for 9.4 percent of the total enlisted personnel but less than 1 percent of the total officer personnel.[3]

During the course of the war 15,850,000 white and 2,150,000 Negro men were examined for military service. Of these totals, more than 700,000 men were rejected because of mental or educational deficiency. Of this number, 45 percent were Negroes. During this same period a total of just under 400,000 illiterates were inducted by the Army. Negroes accounted for more than 40 percent of them, despite the fact that so many Negroes were rejected for similar reasons.

Attitudes within the Army towards the mental abilities of Negroes were influenced not so much by their induction records as by their scores on the Army General Classification Test. Individuals with high scores were placed in groups I or II; III was average; IV was below average; and V represented the least capable group. On the basis of a sample undertaken by the Army in March of 1945, and reported by Stouffer, 28 percent of all Negro enlisted men were in group V and another 45 percent were in group IV. Only 3 percent of the whites were in group V and 23 percent in group IV.[4] Widespread concern with the low test scores of most Negroes helped to obscure the fact that a considerable number actually scored well above the average for white soldiers. About 50,000 Negroes were classified in groups I and II, which meant that they were eligible to attend officer training schools.

In spite of the fact that almost three fourths of the Negro soldiers were in the two lowest mental categories, the Army discharged, prior to demobilization, only 42,000 Negroes on the ground that they did not have the requisite aptitude to perform their military duties effectively. Those who were discharged constituted less than 5 percent of the more than 900,000 enlisted Negro personnel who served during World War II. This is another way of saying that out of every twenty-two Negro soldiers, only one was a clear loss because of a serious deficiency in mental aptitude.[5]

This understates the problem, however, for the Army undoubtedly kept many who should have been discharged if policy and opportunity had permitted. The Army had to make a sizable investment in the form of manpower and other resources to operate the Special Training Units where 254,000 soldiers — half of them Negroes — were brought up to a minimum standard of literacy. Moreover, as we shall see, the Army was never able to develop good Negro divisions because, among other reasons, it could not provide them with enough men who had special skills and average or above average mental ability.[6]

There is no question that on the average the mental aptitude of Negro soldiers was far below that of white troops. Nevertheless, the Army found that most Negroes possessed sufficient mental ability to justify their retention throughout the war. The low mental ability of the Negro was a problem, but it did not prevent their being trained for and assigned to a large number of duties which were crucial for the prosecution of the war.

It would lead too far astray to review all of the evidence bearing on the physical characteristics of whites and Negroes and to assess how these factors affected their military performance during World War II. The most conspicuous and best known difference between the races in this respect was the incidence of venereal disease.

During the first two years of the military build-up, from November, 1940 until October, 1942, both the Army and the Navy rejected individuals who had active gonorrhea or syphilis. This practice led Senator Theodore G. Bilbo of Mississippi to comment, in an interchange with the Deputy Chief of Staff: "In my State, with a population of one half Negro and one half whites . . . the system that you are using now has resulted in taking all the whites to meet the quota and leaving the great majority of the Negroes at home, or they are sent back [from the induction center], because there is the literacy test, and secondly there is the venereal disease. . . . It is resulting in extracting all the white able-bodied men to the Army and leaving the Negroes on our hands." He emphasized that he was anxious for the Army to use this reservoir of manpower by treating men with venereal disease.[7]

Venereal disease was much more prevalent among Negroes than among whites. By August, 1945, Negro registrants accounted for approximately 60 percent of all those rejected for venereal disease. Peacetime studies had found that the prevalence of venereal disease among Negroes was eleven times as great as among whites. The first 2 million Selective Service examinations, between November,

1940 and August, 1941, revealed that less than 18 whites per thousand examined had syphilis, while among Negroes the rate was over 245 per thousand — roughly 14 times as great.

In October, 1942, the Army began to accept a few registrants with uncomplicated gonorrhea. By the following summer the Army was accepting nearly half of the registrants with either gonorrhea or uncomplicated syphilis as their principal physical defect, and the War Department was emphasizing the importance of accepting men with venereal disease to the fullest extent consistent with treatment facilities. As a result of these changing policies, rejections for venereal disease, which had increased to 10 percent of all rejections during late 1942, declined sharply until they reached 1 percent during the first half of 1944. By April 1, 1945, just a few weeks before V-E Day, slightly more than 4.6 million registrants between the ages of eighteen and thirty-seven had been rejected for military service. Venereal disease was responsible for the rejection of about 280,000, or about 6 percent of the total.

Among men on active duty the venereal disease rate was also higher for Negroes than for white soldiers. During the three full years during which the United States was at war, 1942, 1943, and 1944, an average of 15 out of 10,000 troops were noneffective because of venereal disease. The average daily number of noneffectives per 10,000 white personnel was 11; the comparable figure for Negro personnel was 70, or six and one half times as great.

In evaluating the significance of the much higher incidence of venereal disease among Negro troops, it is important to consider what the rates of infection implied for manpower utilization. On the average, during 1942, 1943, and 1944, about 9,000 soldiers were ineffective each day because they were hospitalized or confined to quarters with venereal disease. Of these, over 3,000 were Negroes. Even among the Negroes, however, an average of less than 1 percent were not available for duty on any given day for this reason. The methods of treatment developed during the war — primarily the use of antibiotics — reduced to a very low point the amount of care required to cure venereal infection. Venereal disease, in short, was not a serious military manpower problem.

EMOTIONAL AND BEHAVIOR PROBLEMS

It is not easy to summarize relevant data about the extent to which Negro troops were ineffective because of serious emotional or behavior problems. There was a widespread impression in the Army that Negroes were very much more likely than white soldiers to get into trouble by being absent without leave, getting drunk, pilfering, failing to perform their duties effectively, or any one of numerous possible infractions of military discipline.

Of a total of 2,150,000 Negroes between the ages of eighteen and thirty-seven examined for military service, about 116,000 were rejected because they were so emotionally disturbed that they represented a poor risk, or because they were adjudged to be psychopathic personalities, some of whom had unsatisfactory moral records. This represents a rejection rate of 5.4 percent, which is identical with the rate for whites, of whom 855,000 were rejected on the same grounds out of about 15,850,000 examined. The Negro rate would almost certainly have been higher, however, had not so many of them been rejected because of educational deficiency. The mental and educational qualifications of registrants were examined before their emotional qualifications. Some of those rejected on the former ground would have been rejected for emotional reasons if they had passed previous tests.

During the war the Army discharged a considerable number of men because their emotional problems or infractions of discipline made them a handicap rather than an asset in the prosecution of the war. First, there was a small group of soldiers who got into serious trouble and, as the result of courts-martial, received dishonorable discharges and usually prison sentences. There was a larger group whose infractions were serious but not serious enough to warrant a dishonorable discharge. They were separated from military service with a discharge "other than honorable." The largest group was separated, not for bad behavior, but on grounds of emotional instability. They were medically discharged with a diagnosis of "psychoneurosis."

Negroes accounted for considerably more than their share of soldiers who were discharged dishonorably or without honor, but the number of such soldiers was only a little above 1.5 percent of all Negroes serving, compared with about half of 1 percent in the case of whites. Medical discharges for psychoneurosis were given to the same proportions of white and Negro troops — 2.5 percent.

The numbers involved in serious breaches of discipline were not very large among either white or Negro soldiers. Between 1942 and 1945 just over 10 million enlisted men served in the Army. About 9.2 million were white and 930,000 were Negro. Of these totals, 16,000 whites and 4,000 Negroes received dishonorable discharges. The numbers who received "other than honorable" discharges were considerably greater: 39,000 whites and 11,000 Negroes. A much larger manpower loss occurred through the discharge of men who were found to be emotionally unstable.

About 250,000 white and 26,000 Negro soldiers were separated because they were suffering from a psychoneurosis. The total number of Negroes in the three groups — those discharged dishonorably, without honor, and on a medical certificate with a diagnosis of psychoneurosis — was 41,000. This means that less than five out of every hundred Negro soldiers were adjudged a net loss by the Army because of behavioral or emotional disabilities.

THE NEGRO SOLDIER IN COMBAT

Since, in a war, battle is the pay-off, it is important to consider how effective the Negro was in combat. The riflemen and other members of infantry companies are most constantly engaged in actual fighting. Next come the armored units, artillery, and other heavy weapons supporting groups. Supporting units such as smoke generating companies are sometimes in the forward combat areas. Further back are the divisional and corps service troops — quartermaster, signal, transportation, and others. And in the rear can be found the big supply, transportation, and medical installations which support the men up front. At any point in time not only the men in the line but even those as far back as the division or corps area may be under attack. When enemy bombers seek transports and supply ships that are being unloaded, troops in the communication zone are, as of that moment, exposed to fire. But the exceptions should not obscure the crucial importance of the infantry and armored units which carry the war directly to the enemy.

Evaluation of the Negro's combat record during World War II must be based not only on the performance of the two Negro divisions which the Army trained and sent abroad — the 92nd and the 93rd — but also on the records of many smaller Negro units that participated in various campaigns in Europe and the Pacific. The performance records of the Negro volunteers who were converted to riflemen when General Eisenhower made a special plea for replacements after the break-through of the Germans late in December, 1944 and early January, 1945 must also be reviewed. And the record of Negro airmen cannot be overlooked.

The 93rd Division left the United States for the South Pacific early in 1944, and elements of the Division fought at Bougainville. During the next year and one half the Division was used primarily in noncombat work such as perimeter defense, loading and unloading transports, and similar assignments. During the latter part of the Pacific war elements of the 93rd saw action in Morotai and the Philippines, largely in support of other combat units. Between its activation and V-J Day, the 93rd had four different commanders, and it was never fully tested in the field of battle. Lack of confidence in the division on the part of many who were in a good position to judge prevented it from ever being employed as a unit. The performance of the 25th Regiment, which fought at Bougainville, could be described, at best, as fair. It was definitely below the performance of the white units in the same action.

The 92nd Division became part of General Mark Clark's Fifth Army during the winter of 1944-45, when he was engaged in the difficult operation of pushing the Germans back from their entrenched positions in the Apennines. Although there is evidence that the advance elements performed satisfactorily and that individual enlisted men and officers distinguished themselves during the fighting, the division as a whole had a poor record. The greatest weakness was right at the front, among the men in the rifle squads, who failed to demonstrate the aggressiveness required for carrying the fight to a determined enemy. The Army eventually recognized this by pulling the division out of the line and regrouping it so that the strongest elements were combined with non-Negro units. In evaluating the performance of the 92nd, General Clark stated that its "accomplishments were less favorable than any of the white divisions. On the other hand, there were many instances of individual heroism and successful action by smaller units, such as a company or battalion. . . . Combat support units (tanks, field artillery, anti-aircraft, etc.) in general demonstrated a high degree of efficiency." [8]

If the combat record of the Negro in World War II were appraised solely in terms of the performance of the 92nd and 93rd Divisions, a judgment of unsatisfactory would be necessary. But there is additional evidence. During the early part of the war, the Army planned to form large all-Negro combat units — divisions and regiments. In 1943 the General Staff decided to activate smaller units that could be attached to larger ones. Smaller units would mean important economies in overhead and much greater flexibility. It has been estimated that by the war's end there were at least 4,000 small Negro units. Although many of these units operated in the United States or in the rear areas of overseas theaters, many others were used in direct support of combat units.

Negro units gave strong support to the Iwo Jima landings by bringing ammunition ashore and taking the wounded back to the ships. In the Normandy invasion Negroes had responsibility for the only barrage balloon unit. At Anzio the 387th Separate Engineer Battalion was part of the advance party. Composed of 550 men, it moved almost 2,000 tons a day by hand. During the five months it was at the beachhead, seven officers and sixty-nine enlisted men were killed or wounded. Three Silver Stars were awarded to members of the battalion. Its many duties included operating an asphalt mixing plant, the salvage of steel, repairing submarine cable, operating various sorts of dumps, and helping to clean up the mined areas. Negro port and amphibious companies were attached to the landing parties at Saipan and Okinawa. Negro engineer, chemical, and quartermaster units participated in the initial landings at Salerno. Many Negro ambulance companies served in various campaigns. In fact, Negro units participated in practically all significant actions in the latter part of the war.

The extent to which these small Negro units participated directly in combat or gave important support to combat troops is suggested by considering the units attached to the XVI Corps in the European Theater in April, 1945. These included several field artillery battalions, a chemical smoke generating company, a tank battalion, a quartermaster car company and general service unit, a laundry unit, and a truck company. It has been pointed out repeatedly in the histories of the several divisions and corps that many of these Negro units served in such close association with the combat forces that for all practical purposes they became organic parts of the division or the corps.

Further insight about the Negro as a fighting man can be gained from a quick review of the record of the more than 2,000 volunteers who came forward in response to General Eisenhower's request for infantry replacements after the break-through of the Germans in the Ardennes.

Almost all of the Negro volunteers came from three types of units — engineer, quartermaster, and transportation. Most of them had been truck drivers, longshoremen, construction workers, cargo checkers, or laborers. Not all of these volunteers engaged the enemy before the end of hostilities, since most of them entered the line at the beginning of March, when the Germans were in retreat on many fronts, although still fighting fiercely. Those who have studied their records were impressed by the number of Negroes who gave a very good account of themselves in combat. Others did less well. Apparently the quality of performance depended in large measure on the way in which the Negro troops were organized. Those who fought in platoons alongside of white soldiers did well; most of those organized into larger units, such as companies, had less impressive records. In response to a survey, 84 percent of the white company officers who had commanded Negro volunteers stated that the Negro soldiers in their company had performed "very well" in combat; and 16 percent replied "fairly well." None replied that Negroes had performed "not so well," or "not well at all." [9]

At least passing reference must be made to the 99th Fighter Squadron, which first saw action in North Africa, and the 553rd Fighter Squadron and the 332nd Fighter Group, which participated in the Italian campaign. For some time after the start of the war the Air Corps continued its policy of not training Negroes for combat duties or assigning them to combat units. The Negro community pressed for an opportunity for its members to be trained as combat airmen, and the Air Corps finally agreed to activate the 99th Fighter Squadron.

This was the test case and the first reports from the North African theater were eagerly anticipated. Many senior officers were dubious about the ability of the Negro to fly, and Negro leadership recognized that future policy would largely depend on the performance record of the 99th. Early reports on performance were contradictory. It was to the credit of the senior officers, both in the theater and in the Pentagon, that they refused to jump to quick conclusions. The 99th was given ample opportunity to prove itself and, as the record began to build up, it became increasingly clear that the Negro airmen were performing well. An outstanding record was also achieved by the 332nd. By V-E Day it had flown over 1,500 missions and had completed over 15,000 sorties. In the latter part of the war, the Air Corps was convinced that it was wise to train additional Negroes for flying assignments.

On V-E Day there were more than 500,000 Negro troops overseas and less than 200,000 in the United States. The ratio in overseas assignments was higher than among white troops. No one knows what proportion of the total Negro strength overseas was engaged in combat either on a continuing basis or intermittently — any more than this ratio is known for white soldiers. Many Negroes served under fire with distinction. The answer to the question of whether Negroes were able and willing to fight can be answered with an unequivocal yes.

How well they fought cannot be answered unequivocally. The records of the two Negro divisions were poor. The Army never risked committing the 93rd as a unit and the 92nd did not perform as well as white divisions, even after it was reorganized. Much more favorable reports can be rendered on the performance of the volunteers who became riflemen after the Battle of the Bulge, of the many small units attached to larger white combat groups, and of the Negro air squadrons.

STEREOTYPES AND REALITY

With respect to each of the four indices of ineffective performance used in this chapter, the record of the Negro soldier was less good than that of the white soldier. In every instance, except with respect to discharges for psychoneurosis, his rates of ineffective performance were very much above the average of the white group. Yet, only 9 percent of the Negroes who served were separated for ineffective performance of any type prior to demobilization. Even if an additional allowance is made for those who were ineffective but were not separated prematurely, the conclusion is inescapable that most Negro soldiers were able to perform the duties required of them and some did very well.

At the end of the war many senior officers, however, held to a summary appraisal of the Negro soldier which, in its sharpest form, ran as follows: He was mentally slow and could not be readily taught the skills required to perform military duties effectively. Because many Negroes had venereal disease, their ineffective rate was very high. A high proportion of Negro soldiers presented serious disciplinary problems. Even when they did not challenge authority outright, they frequently engaged in passive resistance which was reflected in very poor performance. According to this view, World War II had proved once again that the Negro would not fight.

One reason for these severe judgments was that segregation spotlighted the Negro's deficiencies. There were many men in the Army, both Negroes and whites, whose personal characteristics or performance left much to be desired. The color of the Negro, however, makes it easy to identify him and segregation made him even more conspicuous. Every Negro who was a poor soldier was unmistakably a Negro. Moreover, since Negro soldiers were segregated, they tended to be concentrated in relatively large numbers. These circumstances made it easy to observe the deficiencies of many Negroes and to attribute them to all.

There was no opportunity during the war for the Army to develop a comprehensive body of facts which would have provided the basis for a balanced judgment about the over-all effectiveness of Negro soldiers. Such facts as did become available were sufficiently negative to enable most white people to conclude that the stereotype of the Negro that they brought from civilian life was justified. The absence of solid facts encouraged many to generalize their personal experiences with some Negro civilians or soldiers and apply the conclusions to all Negro soldiers. Such is the danger of the stereotype.

Human behavior cannot be correctly appraised except on the basis of sound facts, but facts alone will not insure a correct appraisal, for they must always be evaluated. Attitudes and opinions largely determine how individuals weigh and respond to facts. A high proportion of the civilians who became officers during World War II carried into the Army strong opinions about the inferiority of the Negro. The relatively few who were not prejudiced frequently responded with sharp impatience when they ran up against the slow learning ability of the majority of Negroes.

The extent to which even scientifically trained persons had difficulty in assessing Negroes objectively is suggested by the diagnostic conclusions reached by doctors, particularly psychiatrists, in evaluating the ability of Negroes to serve or to continue serving in the armed services. Only 1.4 percent of the white registrants were classified as "psychopathic personalities," while for Negroes the percentage was almost double, 2.6 percent. However, the less invidious category of "psychoneurosis" served as a basis for rejecting 3 percent of the whites and 2 percent of the Negroes. Considering the state of psychiatric knowledge and the speed of the examination, it is questionable whether these differential diagnoses reflected conditions among the Negro and white population, or more nearly bespoke the attitudes of the examining physicians.

With respect to discharges as well as rejections, the Negro was much more likely than the white to be labeled a psychopathic personality rather than a psychoneurotic. Many soldiers who were found to have psychopathic personalities were separated from the Army with an "other than honorable" discharge. More than six times as many white soldiers were separated with medical discharges for psychoneurosis as were given "other than honorable" discharges. In the case of Negroes, however, the proportion was about two to one. Apparently it was difficult for many physicians who had had little or no experience with Negroes to believe that a tall, strong man, especially one who had not seen combat, could be sufficiently distressed by his military experiences to justify the diagnosis of psychoneurosis. It was easier to conclude that the Negro simply was not interested in performing well, that he had character defects which justified an "other than honorable" discharge.[10]

FACTORS AFFECTING NEGRO PERFORMANCE

So far we have evaluated the performance of Negro soldiers without considering why they did conspicuously less well than white soldiers. We have seen also that their performance was by no means as poor as it was often judged to be. The actual deficiencies of many Negroes were often viewed as the innate characteristics of the race. The key to the explanation of the performance of the Negro soldier is to be found, however, in the handicaps he brought with him from civilian life, and in the segregated pattern of his utilization in military service.

There is no question that on the average the mental abilities of the Negroes screened by Selective Service and accepted by the Army were well below the abilities of the whites. But the military attitude toward the Negro soldier was also influenced by the widespread misinterpretation of these facts. It was frequently assumed, just as it had been during and after World War I, that the large numbers of Negro illiterates and the low scores of most Negroes on tests of mental ability reflected low innate intelligence. Actually, as has been shown in *The Uneducated*, the difference between whites and Negroes in these respects was mainly a reflection of the poor homes and inadequate schooling of most Negroes, especially in the South.[11]

The effect of education and other environmental factors is indicated clearly by the very poor showing of Southern Negroes. In the Southeast, which accounted for 60 percent of the 716,000 men rejected for mental or educational deficiency, over 60 percent of those rejected for this reason were Negroes, although Negroes constituted less than 30 percent of the population.[12]

With respect to the problem of venereal disease, there can be little question that the sexual mores of many Negro soldiers differed sharply from those of most members of the white population. But this is not the whole explanation of their venereal disease rates. Among men of both races, the venereal disease rates were much higher for men with little education. However, the Negro rate was higher than the corresponding white rate even among individuals with the same amount of education. Two additional factors should be mentioned. Because Negroes served primarily behind the lines they had more opportunity for sexual intercourse than did combat soldiers. Secondly, as Stouffer has indicated in his careful study of troops in the Mediterranean Theater, a higher proportion of the women with whom Negro soldiers had relations were diseased.[13]

The deprived backgrounds from which most Negroes came and their inferior status in American society affected their performance in many ways. Those who were very poorly educated and who came from the isolated farming areas of the South had little understanding of, or strong identification with, the values for which the United States was fighting. The same circumstances handicapped them in other ways. The largest group of Negroes separated from the Army because of inadequate performance were discharged for "inaptitude or lack of adaptability." Negroes constituted about one third of all those discharged for this reason, and over half the Negroes who were prematurely separated because of inadequate performance received this type of discharge. The kind of behavior which led to this kind of discharge, however, was not so much the result of a character defect as it was of inadequate schooling and lack of familiarity with the requirements of a complex, highly organized society and technology like the Army. Some Negroes did not understand just what they had to do in order to comply with the multitude of regulations required in a disciplined organization, and repeated infractions led ultimately to their discharge. It seems likely that these same circumstances were also partly responsible for the higher proportion of Negroes receiving other than honorable discharges. It must also be remembered that "dumbness" was a habit developed by many Negroes, especially in the South, to protect them in their daily dealings with whites.

The results which the Army secured from the use of its Negro manpower depended not only on the characteristics of Negro soldiers but also on the personnel policies and practices which governed their utilization. It would be difficult to exaggerate the influence of segregation on the training and utilization of Negroes in the Army during World War II. This is not the place to argue whether the Army could have abandoned its traditional practices. In retrospect it is possible to identify what the Army might have done to ease its absorption of so many Negroes and to utilize them more effectively. But it is difficult to criticize the Army strongly for having proceeded with caution in deviating from established practices in the midst of a major conflict. Its principal effort had to be directed to the strategy and logistics required to defeat strong opponents. The consequences of any major change were uncertain and might have been disadvantageous for the successful pursuit of the war.[14]

Segregation affected the performance of Negro troops in at least three major ways. First, assigning men according to color rather than aptitude made it impossible to provide large Negro units with the necessary balance of men with varying aptitudes and skills. Second, the Army had difficulty in developing and assigning the number of capable officers required to get the most out of Negro units. Finally, segregation reduced the opportunities and the motivation of many Negro soldiers.

Much has been made of the poor performance of the two Negro divisions. It is not necessary to argue against this judgment to point out that the divisions were doomed from the start. While the General Staff sought to provide every division with a balance of men with differing mental capacities and skills, it was unable, because of segregation, to do so for the Negro divisions, which had a preponderance of men of low mental aptitude. The same circumstances affected the performance of the Negro who volunteered for combat in the European theater of operations. At this time, seven out of every ten white riflemen in the theater fell into the upper three classes on the Army General Classification Test. But this was true of only three out of ten Negro riflemen in the theater.[15] Here is a clue to why the volunteers who were organized into squads did better than those organized into larger units. The latter could not provide adequate leadership because they had too few men with the requisite skill and aptitude.

The shortage of competent officers, both white and Negro, compounded the difficulties that faced the Army as it sought to make effective use of its Negro manpower. One senior Negro West Pointer and less than 500 Negro reserve officers comprised the total supply of Negro officers at the beginning of mobilization. As the Army expanded, the supply was considerably increased by sending able young Negroes to officer candidate schools. in December, 1941, when the country entered the war, 462 Negro officers were on active duty. A year later there were just under 2,000. By June, 1945, there were almost 5,500. Total Negro officer strength at the end of the war also included almost 500 Negro nurses, 300 Negro flight officers, and over 100 Negro WAC officers.

At the war's end there was one Negro officer for approximately every hundred Negro enlisted men, while the ratio for the Army as a whole was nearly one officer to eight enlisted men. Except for very small units, it was not possible to staff Negro units completely with Negro officers at any time. The scarcity of Negro officers was partly the result of the predominance of men of low ability among Negro troops. On the other hand, only about one out of ten Negro soldiers in the upper two mental classes eventually became an officer, compared to one out of four white soldiers. Moreover, Negro officers were not placed in command over white troops. In addition, many white officers resented their assignment to Negro units. They feared that if they performed well, they might not be reassigned; and if they encountered special difficulties, they would not be excused for failure. In spite of the efforts of higher headquarters to staff Negro units with good officers, there were simply not enough white officers in the Army who combined knowledge, sympathy, and interest. And, as we have seen, there was a serious shortage of good Negro officers, whose efficiency was further reduced by the burdensome practices of segregation.

Because of segregation, many able Negroes had limited opportunity to make full use of their abilities. Regardless of their mental abilities, most Negroes were assigned to quartermaster, engineer, and transportation units where their duties required more strength and stamina than intellectual ability. The lack of opportunity, together with other features of segregation, had a disastrous effect on the morale of the better educated Negroes from the North. In many cases they were deeply resentful of the treatment which they received, both during duty hours within the Army and in off-duty hours in many communities, particularly in the South where strict segregation was enforced. Participation in a war against Fascism intensified their awareness of the gap between basic democratic values and the behavior of the white population toward the Negro. The dominant leadership in the Negro community was determined to use the national emergency to win additional rights and privileges. This struggle, going on while the war was under way, occupied the attention of many of the better educated Negroes, who were most likely to be in leadership positions, and tended to lower their motivation. In many instances it resulted in a deeply negative attitude toward the Army and the war which also affected the men with whom they were associated.

THE EFFECTS OF INTEGRATION

Even during the war Negro leaders, with help from the White House, were able to break through the outer defenses of segregation. Some top Army leaders recognized that there was an irreconcilable conflict between the maintenance of segregation and efficient utilization. World War II, however, came to an end with segregation still strongly entrenched.

After the war, pressure continued for modification and finally for the total abandonment, of the system of segregation. Negro leadership groups, with help from the White

House, again pressed successfully for gains. But it was Korea that finally brought the matter to a head, and it was on the battlefront in Korea that the final break-through came. When General Ridgway replaced General Mac-Arthur as Commander-in-Chief in the Far East, he requested permission from the Department of the Army to proceed with integration, which had gotten under way in the training centers at home in 1950 when the Korean conflict began. He was convinced that only a policy of integration would enable him to make effective use of the Negro soldiers in the theater, as well as of additional Negroes he was likely to receive as replacements. His considered recommendations carried special weight in the Pentagon because he was the only theater commander engaged in fighting.

Military planners realized, on the basis of experience in World War I and World War II, that if the Negro was to fight, he had to fight on an integrated basis. If he did not fight, casualties among white troops would be increased. The top civilian and military leadership of the armed services was able to neutralize Congressional objections to integration by asking opponents whether they wanted to excuse the Negro from battle. The amazing rapidity with which desegregation took place may be illustrated by noting that when the European command was alerted to prepare for it in the summer of 1951, the senior staff suggested that it would require fifty to a hundred years to accomplish. Yet by the summer of 1952 the last vestiges of segregation within that command had been practically wiped out.[16]

In Korea, for the first time, the Negro was permitted to fight as an integrated member of a squad. There is no definitive study of the performance of the Negro in Korea, but there is testimony from a large number of white officers and enlisted men that the Negroes with whom they fought did well. Some performed better than their white comrades, others as well, and still others less well. But the over-all evidence is clear. When given a chance to fight as a member of a balanced unit with competent leadership, the Negro performed satisfactorily.

During the Korean conflict, venereal disease virtually ceased to be a problem for the Army. Instead of a noneffective rate because of venereal disease of approximately 70 per 10,000 Negro troops during World War II, more recent data show a rate of approximately 6 per 10,000. The comparable decline in the rate for white troops has been from 11 to 1 per 10,000. In the 1930's the average soldier who contracted a venereal infection lost 45 days of duty. During World War II there was a sharp decline from an average of 20 days lost per case in 1942, to 6 in 1945. So effective are the antibiotics that the most recent data show no more than one day lost per case. With few exceptions, men are now treated on an out-patient basis for both syphilis and gonorrhea. Early in World War II the noneffective rate because of disease and non-battle injuries was almost 50 percent higher for Negroes than for white troops, primarily because of their much higher incidence of venereal disease. The record for the Korean conflict shows practically no difference in the noneffective rate for disease and non-battle injury between white and Negro troops. The closing of this gap is largely the result of the elimination of venereal disease as a major problem.

Manpower losses sustained in World War II because of soldiers who were discharged dishonorably or without honor, or who were given honorable administrative discharges, or who were separated for disability due to psychoneurosis totaled approximately 4 percent for white personnel and 9 percent for Negro personnel. Because present policy does not permit the Army to collect information based on race, there are no closely comparable data available for the Korean War. However, there has been a striking reduction in the percentage of troops separated on psychiatric grounds — a major cause of manpower losses in World War II. In light of this over-all improvement, there is every reason to assume that a smaller percentage of Negro soldiers have been separated prematurely because of emotional or behavior problems.

Since integration, progress has been made on other fronts. The Negro has been able to achieve noncommissioned officer status comparable to the white soldier. Near the end of World War II only 18 percent of the Negro enlisted strength held the grade of sergeant or better as compared with 31 percent of the whites. At the end of 1955, 28 percent of the Negro enlisted men were in the top three NCO grades, compared with 26 percent of the white soldiers. Negro enlisted men are now being admitted to an increasing number of Army schools, and proportionately more Negroes are now attending these schools than previously. In 1953, the last year for which data are available, Negroes attended 403 out of the Army's 486 courses, or 83 percent; just two years earlier they were attending only 73 percent of the courses. A further reflection of the broadening of opportunity was the 30 percent increase in the proportion of Negro enlisted strength in Army schools between 1951 and 1953.

The success of integration in the Army is in large measure a direct result of the courage and determination of the top civilian and military leadership to see the matter through. But it was also aided greatly by improvements in the quality of Negro recruits. The gains which so many Negroes were able to make on the educational, economic, and social fronts in civilian life were reflected in ever larger numbers of young Negroes entering the services with the aptitudes and skills required for satisfactory military performance.

The problems of the Army during World War II which resulted from the induction of large numbers of illiterate and semi-illiterate soldiers have been further eased in recent years by the raising of mental requirements for military service. During World War II the rejection rate for mental or educational deficiency among Negroes was approximately 15 percent. In 1953 and 1954, the armed services screened nearly 184,000 Negro registrants. In spite of recent gains in Negro education, they rejected over 100,000, or about 55 percent of the total. The armed services argue that in a period of partial mobilization, with adequate numbers available for service, high standards are economical. Others maintain that unless the services learn to cope with marginal manpower during partial mobilization they will again have great difficulty with the problem in the event of full mobilization.

In spite of improvements in the quality of Negro recruits, many Negro soldiers are still handicapped by deficiencies in their prior preparation. But whatever the qualities of the individual Negro, integration has made a tremendous contribution to insuring that he is utilized to his full capacity. He is now evaluated, trained, assigned, and promoted not in terms of color but of his abilities and skills. Integration has made it very difficult to continue to think of the Negro soldier in terms of stereotypes. One of the great dangers of stereotypes is that they inhibit recognition of changing facts. Many who reacted with extreme prejudice against the Negro during World War II were thinking in terms of the experiences of World War I. In the absence of integration it would have been easy for many to see the Negro in 1956 in terms of his attributes and performance during World War II.

The striking gains the Negro has made in recent years in terms of the jobs open to him, the money he earns, and the living conditions he enjoys insure that his children will be better prepared for life than he was. Among the most important advantages that his children will have is military service in fully integrated units. Negro soldiers today are the first Negroes in American history to have equal opportunities to show what they can do. No sensible man can anticipate that the Negro will be able to free himself completely from his past within the next few years. But integration in the services has demonstrated the remarkable ability of both whites and Negroes to adjust to new relations with each other in such a manner that the potential of each can be more fully realized. In demonstrating this fact, the armed services have not only strengthened the nation by strengthening themselves, but have taken the leadership in showing the nation what good will and determination can accomplish.

V: BETTER PREPARATION
FOR WORK

When job opportunities are opened to all men, regardless of color, this does not mean that ability and preparation are no longer relevant in determining who gets the job. If broadened opportunities are to be realized, Negroes must add to their skills and competences. A considerable amount of community and governmental action has been devoted in recent years to increasing the opportunities of the Negro in commerce and industry, particularly in regions outside of the South. Although these efforts have met with increasing success, there is need for them to continue so that opportunities can be opened for Negroes in companies and on jobs from which they are still systematically excluded, in the North as well as in the South. Much effort has also been devoted in recent years to improving the education available to Negroes, especially in the South where the deficiencies have been greatest.

Relatively little attention, however, has been devoted to appraising the whole complex of circumstances that continue to stand in the way of large groups of Negroes assuming their full place in the American economy. Even if discrimination in employment and segregation in schools were suddenly done away with, the problem would not be fully resolved. This may be illustrated most simply by considering a young Negro who leaves his father's farm in the deep South and finds a job as a service station helper in Atlanta or as a laundry worker in New York. He is probably on the road to substantial improvement in his economic position, especially if the prosperity of the last fifteen years continues. Still, there are definite limits to what this former farm laborer will be likely to accomplish in his new urban environment. Poorly educated, he will probably be rejected for military service. With no particular aptitudes or skills and with little opportunity for training, he will not be able to rise above a laborer's job. The crucial question is what will happen to his children and his grandchildren. The answer will depend in no small measure on the drives and opportunities that they have to prepare themselves for work.

THE PROBLEM OF DEVELOPING POTENTIAL

Better preparation for work involves much more than a formal equalization of educational opportunities. For Negroes as for whites, basic preparation for school and for work occurs within the family, the neighborhood, and the community. The habits, the values, and the goals that the child acquires provide the basis for his later accomplishments in school and at work. Because of his history, the American Negro is not prepared in the same way as the white population to take full advantage of the economic opportunities that exist. The Negro must alter many of his values before he will be able to cope effectively with his new situation.

To appraise how Negro potential can be fully developed therefore requires consideration of a whole complex of factors, including the structure and functioning of the Negro family and community and the values and behavior of both Negroes and whites, as well as the present state of and future prospects for his educational and economic opportunities. Each facet is inseparably connected with all of the others. A deficiency in any one area will react adversely on all other areas, just as improvement in any area will lead to cumulative benefits. To speed the development of Negro potential, therefore, requires a concerted and simultaneous attack on all conditions that now impede that development.

The challenges that must be faced and some of the ways in which they can be met may be illustrated by turning again to the young Negro farmer who migrates from the deep South to a Northern city. Even the industrious man on a poor Southern farm is hard put to use his time effectively at certain periods of the year. On the other hand, the Northern worker during the past fifteen years has had the benefit of regular, full-time work. The migrant finds that steady remunerative work soon becomes a regular part of his life. His children will have a much better chance than they would have had on a Southern farm to develop values and habits that will facilitate their later adjustment to an industrial economy.

The urban Negro family in the North is likely to have from four to five times more to spend during the year than the $700 of cash income which is the approximate amount earned by the average Negro farm family. The living conditions of the Northern Negro may not be five times better, but he will have much greater scope for choosing what he buys. Moreover, directly exposed to the wide range of goods and services available, he will probably be stimulated to make greater efforts to raise his standard of living. Urban Negro families are generally much smaller than farm families. Consequently, the higher incomes of the urban families are divided among fewer family members and there is more for each. According to the 1950 Census, married nonwhite women living on farms had an average of about five children each by the time they reached the end of the childbearing period. The corresponding group of urban women had an average of only about two children each.

In a city, the Negro is no longer confined to the very narrow range of jobs available in the rural South. There he could have been a farm laborer or perhaps a lumber mill or road gang worker. The city offers him a much wider range of occupational opportunities, even though his education is limited and his skills few, and in spite of the barriers that remain because of the color of his skin.

Although he will probably have to live in a neighborhood inhabited exclusively by Negroes, during his working day he is likely to have more contact with the white population than he would have had at home. What is more, the quality of these contacts will be quite different than in the South. If he is to make his way in the larger community and if his children are to take advantage of the opportunities that have opened up, this difference is very important.

Northern schools attended by Negroes frequently leave much to be desired, but there can be no question that by moving from the rural South to the urban North, the Negro has made a major contribution to improving the educational preparation of his children. The striking differences in the proportions of Negroes accepted for military service from the North and from the South underline the better schooling available to the Northern Negro — however inferior it remains when compared to the best schooling for whites. The fact that the Northern Negro's sons will have a much better chance to be accepted by the armed forces will also help them prepare themselves more effectively for work.

Further gains of the move from rural South to urban North are the result of the improvement of the Negro's status in the community. Despite occasional outbursts of race conflict in Northern cities and many restrictions on true equality, the Negro is much closer to being a full citizen in the North than he has been or will be for many years to come in the South. It would be hard to exaggerate the importance of this factor, not only for the migrant Negro, but even more so for his children as they seek their rightful place in American society.

The rapid movement of Negroes to Northern cities represents a substantial contribution to solving the problem of developing Negro potential. This contribution is by no means confined to the advantages accruing to the Negroes who migrate. The Negro who remains in the South also benefits. His economic opportunities are improved by the draining off of part of the surplus labor supply. The more fully the Negro is integrated into Northern communities, the greater is the pressure against segregation in the South. Eventually, the reduction in the Negro population in the South will weaken segregation, for discrimination tends to be most severe where the Negro population is largest compared to the white population.

It would be idle to imagine, however, that the migration of Southern Negroes to Northern cities will provide an adequate answer to the problem. In the first place, not all Negroes can move to the North. In the second, as has been seen in previous chapters, even in the North the Negro suffers from serious inequalities of opportunity. Because inequality is so deeply imbedded in the past, it will take considerable time, even under the best of circumstances, for the Negro to gain equal status with the white population. The speed with which this goal is reached will depend on the extent to which those who seek its accomplishment become aware of the problems that must be solved. It is the responsibility of the white community to provide equality of opportunity, both educational and economic. The leaders of the Negro community, of course, must continue to press for treatment according to merit rather than color. But this is only the beginning of their responsibility. They must convince their fellow Negroes that equality cannot be bestowed; it must be earned. Negroes must learn how to utilize the opportunities now open to them. Only if they do so will they achieve the equality they seek.

THE INFLUENCE OF THE FAMILY

Preparation for work begins in earliest childhood. When a young Negro has an opportunity to apply for a good job, his willingness to compete for it and his prospects of securing it depend on his earlier development and preparation for work. It is hard to exaggerate the importance of the home in this connection. As the National Manpower Council recently pointed out, "It is not possible to acquire skill, and surely not possible to acquire a high level of skill, unless one is motivated to do so and puts forth real effort."[1] Few become skilled workers by accident. Although relatively little is known about the growth, during the formative years, of basic values, including values connected with work, there can be no question that the child develops these values largely as a result of his relations to his parents and other key persons in his environment. If the father hates his work and the mother fails to plan for the future, these considerations will be reflected in the later work attitudes and behavior of their offspring.[2]

The family structure of Negroes has long been subjected to serious stresses and strains. Millions of Negroes leave their home communities during their formative years and must sink roots in new and different communities. Many family units are disrupted, temporarily or permanently, by migration. Residential restrictions in the large urban centers of the North are a serious handicap to family life, for they imply poor housing, inadequate recreational facilities, and all other blights of slum areas.

Moreover, a disproportionately large number of young Negroes are brought up in homes which the father has deserted or in other situations where major responsibility for the continuance of the family unit centers around the mother and her relatives. According to the 1950 Census, over one third of the Negro women who had ever been married were no longer married or no longer living with their husbands. This was true of only one fifth of the white women. The absence of the father, or the fact that he often plays a secondary role when present, makes it difficult for the young Negro male to develop a strong positive motivation for work. The father's absence also puts additional stress on the mother who must work to support herself and her children. The 1950 Census found that about 35 percent of the Negro mothers under the age of forty-five were in the labor force while this was true of only 19 percent of white mothers.

This problem has been dealt with very succinctly by E. Franklin Frazier in these terms:

The incidence of desertion on the part of the male . . . is much greater among Negroes than among other racial or ethnic elements in the population. . . . Since family disorganization is so widespread, the family environment of a large number of Negro children is precarious and fragmentary. . . . Because of the lack of discipline, the children in such homes never acquire the most elementary habits in regard to cleanliness or even as to eating. . . . They do not even acquire the domestic work skills necessary to make a living. . . .

Negro children from disorganized families often exhibit little interest in the knowledge and the skills provided by the public schools because it has little or no meaning for them in terms of their family background. . . . The lack of family discipline and a failure of the disorganized family to provide models . . . of the values of the community are partly responsible at least for the irregular work habits and lack of ambition among many Negro youths. . . . The mitigation of this problem must await those changes in the Negro and American society which will enable the Negro father to play the role required of him.[3]

But even if the Negro child grows up in a normal family and has good relationships with both parents, it is often difficult for him to develop proper attitudes and habits for the world of work. Most Negro parents have had to work hard most of their lives at jobs which command little esteem, are often extremely unpleasant, and provide no more than a subsistence wage. Many Negroes are likely to feel embittered or resigned about their work, and these attitudes will eventually carry over to their children. The Negro child, moreover, is also likely to respond to the attitudes of the dominant white population toward the work role of his race. Seeing his elders holding down poor jobs and sensing that the white community takes this for granted, the Negro child is not likely to develop high aspirations for himself. Only as increasing numbers of their own race rise in the world of work will more young Negroes develop the motivation necessary to prepare themselves properly to compete for the better jobs.

THE HOME AND THE SCHOOL

The home and the family also help to determine the young Negro's performance in school. In seeking to correct the errors that were initially made in interpreting the low scores of Negroes on Army intelligence tests in World War I, psychologists emphasized that there was probably no significant difference in the genetic potential of Negroes and white persons. Insufficient attention has been paid, however, to the ways in which cumulative environmental handicaps can result in gross differences in *developed* potential between the vast majority of Negroes, who grow up under unfavorable conditions, and the many white children who grow up under more favorable circumstances.

The school and the home always stand in a reciprocal relationship to each other. When children first enter school, there are great differences in their ability to profit from it, resulting in large part from their preschool experiences. The child who begins school with a meager store of facts about the world around him, with a limited vocabulary, with no sense of the pleasures to be found in learning, is under a handicap that he is never likely to fully overcome. It is next to impossible, even for a skillful teacher, to stimulate students to develop their latent potential unless parents take a positive or at least neutral attitude toward the schooling process. Although many Negro parents are aware of the handicaps they have suffered because of poor schooling and therefore place great store on a good education for their children, there are many others who do not have a positive attitude toward their children's schooling. It is not easy for a Negro child to respond enthusiastically to school when there is nothing in his home or community environment to feed the interests that have been awakened. Books are hard to come by, but even more enervating is the absence of sympathetic understanding on the part of the elders of what goes on in school and its value for the future adjustment of the child. Many white children, especially boys, are strongly motivated to work hard in school, in part because they realize the importance of schooling for their future work. But since the Negro boy is likely to have a limited occupational objective, he is less likely to have this stimulus to do well in school.[4]

It is too much to ask of the school that it make up for all of the deficiencies in the home and the community. Yet the fact that so many Negro children come from deprived families who live in disadvantaged neighborhoods presents a special challenge to the school. If it is to accomplish its primary mission of instruction, the school must provide special support to compensate for the major values lacking at home. Unfortunately, in most urban communities the public schools that serve Negroes have neither the physical nor the personnel resources to meet their primary responsibilities, let alone the ability to cope with these additional ones.

Still other circumstances handicap the Negro student. Segregation, whether in law or in fact, creates school classes composed exclusively of children who come from disadvantaged homes. If most students are slow learners, there is little incentive for the potentially good student to excel. A Negro student who attends an interracial school in the North may encounter other psychological obstacles. His teachers are usually white. This fact alone may inhibit the quality of his performance. The Negro student may be further inhibited by repeated failures to meet the competition of better prepared white students. The combined effects of poor homes, poor neighborhoods, and poor schools on the intellectual development of the Negro have been documented in Chapter III, where it was pointed out that even in the North, the potential of Negro children is seriously stunted as early as the eighth grade.

THE ARMED FORCES AND SKILL DEVELOPMENT

How the disadvantages of home and school limit the later opportunities of Negroes to acquire skill can be dramatically illustrated by reference to the armed forces. Confronted with the necessity of using men who serve for only a short period to operate and service a highly complex military technology, the armed forces cannot make their advanced training courses available to everyone whom they induct or enlist. They must select those most likely to cope quickly and effectively with the demands of training. They have found that those who can most easily profit from advanced training are men who fall in the upper half of the test score distribution for mental aptitude. Table 15 shows this distribution for white and Negro men examined for military service in a recent year. Data are shown for the United States as a whole and for the Third Army Area, which consists of Alabama, Florida, Georgia, Mississippi, North Carolina, South Carolina, and Tennessee. The table shows that only 18 percent of all Negroes and less than 10 percent of the Negroes in the Third Army Area were in the upper three groups, compared to 65 and 48 percent, respectively, of the whites.

The following paragraph from the National Manpower

TABLE 15. PERCENT DISTRIBUTION AMONG MENTAL GROUPS OF
MEN EXAMINED FOR MILITARY SERVICE, DECEMBER, 1951

MENTAL GROUPS	WHITE		NEGRO	
	U.S.	3rd Army Area	U.S.	3rd Army Area
I	6.3	2.9	0.4	0.1
II	24.0	13.3	3.5	0.8
III	34.3	31.6	14.1	8.1
IV	31.3	40.8	52.3	46.8
V	4.1	11.4	29.7	44.2

Source: Adjutant General's Office, Department of the Army.

Council's *A Policy for Skilled Manpower* points up the serious loss of opportunity that many Negroes experience because they cannot qualify for advanced training in service schools:

The elaborate training offered by the armed forces opens up areas of training and work experience to many who, in civilian life, would be barred from such training and work because of discriminatory practices. Some men, of course, are so severely handicapped by lack of proper education and training prior to their entering service that they cannot be given technical training. The fact that military training in many cases provides the impetus for new and higher occupational goals underlines its importance for men from depressed farm areas, for Negroes, and for others who do not have equal access to civilian training opportunities.[5]

Even more serious than the fact that most Negro servicemen cannot qualify for advanced training is the failure of many Negroes even to be accepted for military service. The preceding chapter pointed out that more than half of all Negroes examined for military service in 1953-54 were rejected on mental grounds. To the armed services it is a

waste of the taxpayer's money to take a young man with
only a few years of elementary education and try to trans-
form him into an efficient soldier, particularly in a military organization in which technical skill has now become
the key to efficiency.

A major disability of the young Negro in the world of
work is his lack of intimate knowledge of the values and
behavior of the white population with whom he is in frequent contact. His ability to cope with the problems presented by working with whites depends largely on the opportunities he has had in his formative years to live in
close association with members of the white race. The
armed forces provide him with an excellent chance to ex-
pand such experience in living and working with whites as
he has earlier acquired. Hence, rejection for service represents a much greater loss for the Negro than for the
white man.

PREPARATION FOR SKILLED WORK

By the time the Negro youth reaches adulthood, he is
likely to be triply handicapped in his preparation for work
by experiences at home, in school, and in connection with
service in the armed forces. But these do not exhaust his
special disabilities. Preparation for work normally continues long after the individual gets his first job. For instance, the great majority of the skilled workers and foremen in our economy acquire their skills gradually, over
the course of many years at work. Typically, the worker
begins with a low-level job and moves up as he accumu-
lates competence that he gains by moving from one assignment to another, frequently from one employer to another.
In this process he is usually aided, at one time or another,
by informal or formal training, either in the plant or at a
school.

To acquire skills in this way, the worker must first be able to get the right type of job at which he can learn enough to move on to a slightly different job which is somewhat more skilled, more responsible, which pays somewhat better, and from which he can move again. Employers are becoming increasingly demanding about the educational qualifications of young people whom they hire for such break-in jobs. Especially in the North, but also increasingly in the South, high school graduation is a prerequisite. This is the natural result of the rising educational level of the population and the increasing complexity of our industrial technology. A generation or two ago, a man with negligible formal education could become a skilled worker. Today, participation in the industrial process requires of the worker not only basic literacy but a fairly high level of ability to deal with words and figures. The prospective employee must first be able to cope with a complicated application form. On the job, he must be able to follow written instructions, to read the bulletin board, to keep various kinds of records. If he advances very far, he must also be able to master considerable technical knowledge.

The inferior quantity and quality of their educational preparation makes it difficult for Negroes even to be considered for jobs from which one can later advance. Poor preparation is not the only reason why the Negro has encountered serious difficulty in breaking into the area of skilled work, but it does add to the obstacles created by racial discrimination. The informal route to skilled and supervisory work, therefore, is a rocky road for the young Negro. On the formal route, through apprenticeship training, his obstacles are perhaps even greater. Apprenticeship is most important in the building trades. Here the unions exercise a high degree of control over the admission of apprentices, which has frequently been used to exclude Negroes. In the South, many unions have excluded Negroes entirely from the union and therefore from skilled work, or have forced them into all-Negro locals, where they have limited rights and opportunities.

In spite of the important gains that the Negro has made outside of the South in recent years through the opening of wider economic opportunities, his progress has been slow in the case of apprenticeship training. Many locals in the North continue in one way or another to bar Negroes from apprenticeship. Many Negroes have been able, however, to acquire skills informally. Usually a Negro is taken on as a helper and given more responsibility as he learns one facet of the job after another. Although he may become a journeyman through this pick-up process, he is not as likely to acquire the same rounded knowledge of his trade as are workers who successfully complete a formal apprenticeship.

The difficulties encountered by the Negro in gaining entrance into apprenticeship programs reflect not only overt discrimination but also his inadequate preparation. Both trade unions and employers have become concerned over the high costs involved in the heavy attrition of trainees from formal apprenticeship programs. One major reason for the failure to complete apprenticeship is the difficulty many young people find in completing their related school instruction, which generally totals at least 144 hours a year of formal classroom work. Most apprenticeship programs, therefore, will now accept only those trainees who have graduated from high school with a reasonably good record.

Once again, his poor educational preparation proves a serious handicap. It was noted in Chapter III that even

among those Negroes who complete high school successfully, many have not taken the college preparatory course.
Although it is surely not necessary for a student to take the
full college preparatory program to become a skilled
worker, he needs sound preparation in the fundamentals
of mathematics and science if he is to cope later on with
the related instruction of most apprenticeship programs.
Most vocational programs attempt to provide their students with such preparation. But in those which have a
high proportion of Negro students, the instruction is neces-
sarily geared to the low learning ability of the majority.
Moreover, the courses offered are very likely to be limited
to the kinds of work which have been open to Negroes
traditionally. Consequently, the able Negro student is not
likely to get adequate high school preparation for becoming a skilled worker unless he enrolls in the academic
program.[6]

There are still other circumstances that interfere with
the young Negro's becoming a skilled worker. It has been
pointed out that to acquire the necessary skills and competence a man must make a real effort over a long period,
both in school and later during his apprenticeship or on
the job. Many young people are unwilling to make this
effort because they hold manual work in low esteem. For
them, white collar work has more prestige, even though
it may not pay as well. This attitude is reinforced by the
fact that preparation for skilled work usually requires a
substantial sacrifice of immediate financial rewards. Apprentices earn less than semi-skilled production workers
and frequently even less than unskilled workers. There are
many laborer's jobs which lead no place but which pay
more than many break-in jobs in manufacturing.

The low prestige of manual work and the necessity of

postponing rewards undoubtedly deter many young people of both races from training for skill. But these factors are probably more significant for Negroes than for whites. For decades the Negro had little basis for a rational planning of his preparation for work. He set himself either no goals or badly skewed goals. As a result of his background, the ambitious young Negro is even more likely than the white youth to scorn skilled work and to overestimate the importance of achieving status through white collar or professional employment.

PREPARATION FOR THE PROFESSIONS

Negroes are even more poorly represented among scientists and professionals than they are among skilled workers. In 1950 the proportion of Negro men in professional and related occupations was only about one fourth the proportion among white men. Actually, the Negro's role in the professions is even more limited than this figure indicates. Until recently, most Negro professionals were either teachers or clergymen. This is still true of the South today. In these occupations, Negroes do not compete with whites. They provide professional services for members of their own community and are able to find employment even if their preparation and competence is below that of white professionals.

This situation is now changing rapidly. In the North, at least, the well-trained Negro can find employment in a variety of fields in the larger community. This is especially true in the sciences and engineering where, for a number of years, the demand for qualified persons has been much larger than the supply. The professionally trained Negro is still discriminated against by many employers. Yet the speed with which the professional employment of Negroes will increase in the future will depend more on the number of Negroes who complete professional training than on breaking down additional barriers to their employment. Agencies engaged in broadening the economic opportunities for Negroes have found in recent years more job openings at the professional level than fully qualified Negroes to fill them.

Increasing the number of Negroes who receive college and graduate training and improving the quality of higher education for Negroes are, therefore, the most important ways of insuring that a larger number will be employed at the professional level. But this goal, like so many others, is difficult to achieve. Very few Negroes complete high school with the necessary qualifications to enter a college which maintains reasonably high standards. In addition, many of the best graduates from Negro high schools in the South shy away from seeking admission to good interracial colleges, even when offered scholarship aid. Most of them attend one of the segregated colleges in the South. The weakness of many of these institutions is well known. They have had difficulty in finding competent faculty members and have seldom been able to maintain good libraries, laboratories, and other basic facilities. They have also been forced to gear their instruction to the abilities of their students, most of whom come from mediocre high schools and are therefore unable to pursue a rigorous college program. These institutions have done the best they can with the resources and students they have. They have performed a valuable service for the Negroes of the South, but the fact remains that their graduates are often not prepared to compete for jobs on an equal basis with white college graduates.

For a long time the well-qualified Negro high school graduate had difficulty in obtaining admission to the private colleges and universities outside the South. In recent years, however, these institutions, having become aware of the advantages of a varied student body, often seek out such Negro applicants and are even willing to accept some whose qualifications may be questionable. For the Negro to be able to compete successfully for work at the professional level involves, therefore, much more than improving his opportunities for securing a higher education. Changes are required all along the line — at home, in his community, in his elementary school and high school. Only as these changes are brought about will he be able to develop his potential and be motivated to do so.

Nevertheless there are serious problems in higher education for Negroes which can be attacked directly. One of these is the inadequate financing of Negro colleges in the South. Another is the cost of higher education to the Negro family. A college education is becoming increasingly expensive, in terms of both tuition and maintenance, and Negro parents are generally far less able to support their children through college than are white parents. Many able Negro boys and girls never plan to attend college for this reason. And many of those who do attend are severely handicapped by having to earn their full tuition and living expenses.

For the Negro who attends an interracial college, participation in extracurricular activities presents another hurdle. Much of the preparation for a professional life is derived, not from books alone, but from the abilities that one develops through experience in dealing with people in social situations. Until recently the Negro was cut off almost completely from normal relations with his white fellow students, but this pattern, too, has begun to change. The need for change in social relations points to the importance of breaking down residential segregation. The more young Negroes have an opportunity to live in close and continuing contact with the white population, the more likely they are to develop similar values. Shared experience is a prerequisite for true equality of opportunity.

THE NEGRO COMMUNITY AND THE
DEVELOPMENT OF NEGRO POTENTIAL

At least three basic conclusions emerge from this chapter. One is that while expanding economic opportunities are essential, new opportunities by themselves will have little value unless Negroes are adequately prepared to take advantage of them. Another is that preparation for work is a cumulative process that begins in earliest childhood and involves the total life of the individual, not only his formal education and training. The final conclusion is that much of the responsibility for improving the Negro's preparation for work falls on the Negro community itself.

The recent growth of new employment opportunities for Negroes is important in itself and even more because of its consequences for the future. The younger generation of Negroes cannot be expected to invest heavily in developing their abilities unless they can see a reasonable chance of putting their training to use. Moreover, every improvement in the financial base for a good family life contributes in many ways to the fuller development of the innate potential of the younger generation. It is, therefore, important for Negro leaders to continue to strive against discriminatory employment practices. But, in addition to striving to remove the remaining barriers, they must allocate time and effort to make Negro youth aware of the new opportunities so that they will prepare themselves adequately to take advantage of them.

It is not easy for a group that has been so seriously discriminated against and that has been forced to exist on the periphery of society to become quickly aware of major changes in its condition. The Negro community has developed deep-seated, traditional ways of thinking about how its members can best prepare for work and life. We have noted the importance ascribed to teaching and to the ministry, and the deprecation of manual work. These are not irrational patterns, but practical adaptations to the discrimination that Negroes have long encountered. However, it would be unfortunate if these approaches continued to dominate now that conditions have begun to change. The young Negro today needs to know not only about the new opportunities which already exist, but also about those likely to be opened up by the time he completes his education. In short, there is a major challenge to be faced in the counseling and guidance of Negro youth. This challenge cannot be met through a few brief sessions with a school counselor. It requires, rather, changes in the basic attitudes of parents, teachers, and the Negro community at large.

Recognition on the part of Negroes of the need for better preparation for work will be of little avail unless better preparation can be secured. The growing importance for an individual to acquire a high school or college diploma for entrance into a better job has been repeatedly stressed. Better preparation for work means not only that more Negroes must complete high school and college, but also that the quality of education they receive must be vastly improved. Within the last fifteen years compulsory military service has come to represent an important new institution that helps to prepare men for work and life. The importance of this development has not been fully grasped either by

Negroes or whites. Military service, however, has special significance for the Negro population. Since the armed forces are fully integrated, they can provide the young Negro with a unique opportunity to gain experience in living and working as an equal with whites.

It would be a serious error, however, to think of better preparation for work solely in terms of college, high school, and the armed forces. At every stage in the development of the young person, what can still be accomplished in the future is limited by the foundations built in the past. Negro achievement in high school is poor not only because the high schools are poor but because Negro students were poorly instructed in elementary school. The achievement of Negro children during the elementary grades is low because they bring to school the handicaps growing out of a childhood characterized by poverty, family instability, inferior social status, and isolation from the white community. There is evidence that the intellectual potential of Negro children growing up in deprived neighborhoods is already seriously stunted well before they reach school age. Improving the preparation of Negroes for work involves, therefore, fundamental changes in many aspects of Negro life. By the same token, however, any improvement in the education, work, or life of the Negro will enable the present generation, and more particularly future generations, to be better prepared for work.

These considerations suggest that it is important for leaders of the Negro community to assess carefully the priorities they assign to various kinds of efforts to speed the assimilation of Negroes into American society. Since all the factors impeding the realization of this goal are closely related to each other, it is important to seek improvements at every point. Nevertheless, recent developments may call for some adjustment in emphasis. Thus, more attention should be paid to preparing young Negroes for the new employment opportunities that have been opened up and that are likely to become open in the near future. The Negro community must do more than it has in the past to help its own members adjust to changing conditions.

Negro leaders have concentrated on breaking open areas of employment from which their members have previously been barred, and have stressed high prestige jobs, such as the professions. The continued importance of these efforts cannot be denied. On the other hand, there are never many opportunities at the top of the occupational ladder, even for whites. It may be that more emphasis should be placed on helping larger numbers of Negroes to achieve more easily realizable occupational advances. The importance of such a goal is underlined by the fact that the early environment of many Negroes continues to severely restrict their later development. Even modest advances in the living conditions of Negro families may make a significant contribution to preserving the potential of their children. This suggests, in turn, that it is imperative to concentrate efforts on improving Negro education at elementary and secondary school levels. Contrary to a widespread impression, this is an important task in the North as well as the South. Because the ability of Negroes to profit from higher education is severely restricted by deficiencies in their prior preparation, such an emphasis may also be the quickest and best way to insure a substantial improvement in the accomplishments of Negroes in higher education.

Finally, it must be recognized that the Negro cannot suddenly take his proper place among whites in the adult world of work if he has never lived, played, and studied with them in childhood and young adulthood. Any type of segregation handicaps a person's preparation for work and life. The Supreme Court took cognizance of this fact in its school decision and therefore called for integration. Yet conditions in many Northern cities indicate that segregation does not always require legal sanction. Indeed, residential segregation is often more rigid in the North than in the South. Only when Negro and white families can live together as neighbors, when Negro children and white children can play together, study together, go to the same church — only then will the Negro grow up properly prepared for his place in the world of work.

VI: LESSONS FOR
MANPOWER POLICY

It is never sensible or right for a nation to waste valuable human resources through failure to develop or utilize them. The consequences of such waste are a lower level of national strength and individual well-being.

In a time of international tension, such as now confronts the United States and is likely to continue for a long period, wastage of national resources can only result in a more vulnerable security position. Moreover, the frustration and stunting of individuals who cannot develop or utilize their full capacity involves costs to the nation which transcend military strength. The outcome of the struggle between the free world and Soviet Russia for the minds and hearts of millions of men who are not yet committed will depend on actions, not speeches. The hungry and the downtrodden will not be taken in by propaganda barrages. Their decision will be based upon what actually happens to the men, women, and children who live under the different systems. In a period of such challenge every nation must declare for what it believes and be counted for how it acts.

STRATEGY FOR DEVELOPING POTENTIAL

A study of the more effective utilization of 15 million Negroes, roughly 10 percent of the nation's population, has significance not only within the preceding context but also because it may contribute to the shaping of a strategy for developing latent manpower potential wherever it exists. The first and perhaps most significant finding emerging from this study is that improvements in the position of the Negro occurred primarily as the direct outgrowth and consequence of forces unleashed in the market place. They were not primarily a result of alterations in our social and political thinking and behavior. It is fashionable for critics of contemporary American life to point with disdain to our national preoccupation with the material aspects of life — the production of ever greater quantities of goods and the desire of so many to secure an ever larger amount of these goods. But this precise state of affairs has led to marked improvements in the position of American Negroes. Their higher standard of living since 1940 has been in large part a direct outgrowth of the growing demand for labor in American towns and cities. Except for this quickening of the economic pace, which has resulted in fifteen years of uninterrupted economic expansion, it is questionable indeed whether the Negro would have been able to reach his present place on the economic scale. Poverty cripples while prosperity heals. Vestiges of the suffering endured during slavery and the hardships wrought by segregation cannot be eradicated by money alone. Nevertheless, the best hope for the Negro's speedy and complete integration into American society lies in the continuation of a strong and virile economy in which his labor is needed and his skills and capabilities rewarded.

Although the review of the educational preparation of the Negro pointed out significant gains during recent decades, the same figures highlighted the extent to which the education of the Negro still lags behind that of the white man. Not only does the Negro continue to remain in school for fewer years, but, even more important, the quality of his schooling is still far below that of the white child. If the Negro is to participate fully in the economy at every level instead of only at the bottom rung, his education must still undergo substantial improvements. Increasingly, a high school diploma, or a college or advanced degree, is required of those who seek one of the better positions in the economy.

The study of the Negro soldier illuminated the impact of segregation on the utilization of Negro manpower in World War II. The review of the integration that took place during the Korean hostilities pointed up the gains that followed when opportunities were broadened. Perhaps the most important lesson of the integration experience is that the manner of the change was largely responsible for its success. Only the top civilian and military leaders could assume responsibility for eliminating segregation. Once they did, many of the fears, anxieties, and uncertainties which had been diffused throughout the organization, from the noncommissioned officer to the senior theater commander, disappeared. It was no longer necessary for the individual to determine for himself the wisdom of the move or his willingness to participate in it. From the viewpoint of mobilizing support for speedy action, hierarchical systems such as the armed services are at a great advantage. Clearly, however, the new policy would never have been embarked upon nor would it have succeeded unless there was already some support for it throughout the organization and in the society at large.

Negro leaders must play a vital role in preparing the Negro to take full advantage of the new opportunities opening up in American military and civilian life. They must first be interested in, and appreciative of, the significant changes that are taking place. They must develop appropriate methods for making those changes known to the Negro population. And, most important, they must develop appropriate means of helping parents and youngsters prepare for broadened opportunities. The intellectual and moral challenge is severe. Many favorite projects and beliefs must be discarded or significantly altered. Much imagination will be required to fashion appropriate new instruments for more effective interpretation and guidance.

But the Negro leadership cannot do the entire job by itself. White leaders must do their part in making it possible for the Negro to become a fully integrated citizen. This means that they will have to help the Negro become part of the community from his birth, and not have him wait until he enters military service. The Negro needs the opportunity to grow up, go to school, play, and work together with the white population.

FUTURE TRENDS: THE ECONOMY

Although it is difficult enough to unravel the skein of the Negro's history during the past half century, it is far more difficult to estimate what is likely to occur during the decade or two ahead. Some of the following estimates of the future will be proved incorrect, but the chance of error may be reduced by using as a guide the principal lines along which past developments have taken place. On the basis of the analyses presented in the preceding chapters, four such lines of development may be discerned: trends in the economy, in public education, in the Federal government, including the armed services, and in the community at large.

Although, during the past fifteen years, the economy has

not experienced any significant decline in the levels of output or employment, it cannot be concluded that the economy is now immune from such declines or that the future will bring uninterrupted growth. On the contrary, the study of long-run trends suggests that at some time within the next few years there is likely to be a period of reduced business activity which will probably be much more moderate than the great depression of 1929-33. Although there is no certainty that a major economic disorganization cannot again occur, there are many reasons for contending that future business declines will be moderate. As the passage of the Full Employment Act of 1946 so clearly indicated, both major parties are now committed to the principle that the Federal government should use its full power to help the economy regain its health whenever necessary.

Trends in the level of economic activity have direct and striking pertinence for the Negro: the longer the period of prosperity the more secure he can make his position in the economy and the less he has to fear from a period of decline. With the passage of every year the Negro acquires greater seniority in those areas of the economy where he has recently been able to obtain employment for the first time. Although job security is greater for those who are members of unions that have stringent seniority provisions in their contracts, even those who are not protected by collective bargaining agreements become increasingly secure the longer they hold their jobs. Over the past decade or two, many nonunion employers have established personnel policies that consider seniority when men are released as well as when they are promoted. Although it is hard to predict the impact of a serious depression on these policies, it is unlikely that the Negro would be singled out for differential treatment where such policies are in force, especially where they are written into contracts with unions.

The revolution in Southern agriculture will undoubtedly continue, with the result that there will be much less demand for unskilled Negro labor in the future. It is reasonable to postulate, therefore, a continuing migration of Negroes from the rural areas of the South. Those who remain will be particularly handicapped because they will be older and less well educated, on the average, than those who leave. Yet, there are some reasons for hope. The President is committed to the development of a constructive program to help the depressed economic areas of the country, and the Congress has also demonstrated an interest in this problem. A recent report of the Joint Committee on the Economic Report stressed the need for several kinds of actions to help low income farmers. These included increased credit, intensive technical assistance, and the development of individual plans to improve family farms. The report emphasized the individual farmer's needs for encouragement and guidance as he seeks to fulfill his plan. In addition, the Committee suggested three further lines of action: "(1) Encouragement of off-farm employment by development of new industrial location within the area; (2) assistance of farm families willing to migrate to other areas and who possess definite job opportunities in the new location; (3) provision for greater opportunity for rural people to obtain training for nonfarm occupations."[1] If these and similar constructive actions are taken, the most handicapped Negroes — those born and brought up in the depressed agricultural areas of the Southeast — can look forward to an improved opportunity to secure a better living from the land, or to make a successful transition to urban industry.

There is no reason to doubt the continuation of the rapid industrialization of the South. This industrialization has helped the Negro to improve his economic position, even though he has rarely been able to gain a firm footing in the manufacturing labor force. Whether he will be able to do so in the years ahead is difficult to foretell. Breakthroughs which have already occurred on the periphery of the South and occasionally in the deep South provide some ground for optimism. In these instances Negroes have been hired as production workers and have had an opportunity to move up the ladder as they acquired skill on the job.

The time is near when the South will have to make a major decision. Negroes represent approximately one fourth of the population of the South. It is indeed questionable whether the South will be able to keep pace with the rest of the country if it continues to lose its most competent and best-trained Negroes. At present, a young Negro who has acquired skills in the armed services and comes back even to such a metropolitan center as Atlanta finds it difficult to obtain a job which uses his skills. Before long his availability is made known to employment exchanges north of the Mason-Dixon Line, and he is likely to be on his way, lost to the South forever. Other costs are also implicit in the maintenance and operation of a segregated system of employment. Such a system inevitably results in excessive overhead and faulty utilization practices since men must be assigned primarily according to their color rather than the needs of the plant. The South will have to give up the luxury of maintaining segregation in the work place and begin to make progressive moves to abandon it, if it is to strengthen its position in the never-ceasing competition for new plants.

Since the long-run trend of economic activity is definitely upward, the Negro can anticipate greater opportunities for employment, particularly outside of the South. It will be easier for him to get a job and it will be easier for him to be promoted on the basis of merit. There are strong indications that American industry will be able to absorb all the skilled workers who are trained. The unskilled Negro, however, will be vulnerable. During the next decade improvements in machinery, including advances in automation, may well lessen the demand for such labor. Improved opportunities for the Negro in American industry will depend in no small measure, therefore, upon his ability to meet the demands of employers for men with a high level of education and skill.[2]

It is difficult to predict the extent to which Negro women will be able to improve their economic position by gaining access to new occupations and by rising in them as they gain knowledge and experience. Since 1940 few Negro women in the South have been able to obtain work in manufacturing, clerical, and sales work. In the North, too, their opportunities are still severely limited. One important area of employment may present greatly increased opportunities for Negro women in both the North and the South over the next decade — the field of health services. Today many hospitals in the North could not operate without the help of Negro nurses and auxiliaries. There is also scattered evidence in the South that exceptions to segregation are being made in the health fields for properly qualified Negro women. An expanding economy with rising personal incomes will bring increasing demands for social and health services. On the other hand, a rapid integration of students in Southern school systems would undoubtedly reduce the opportunities of Negro girls to obtain teaching positions, at least temporarily.

In sum, if the general upward trend of the economy continues, the position of the Negro should also continue to improve. There are, however, certain danger points: in a depression, all Negroes would be more vulnerable; with advances in automation, the unskilled Negro will be in a weakened position; the jobs of Negro women teachers in the South could be jeopardized by quick integration of school systems. But, on balance, an expanding economy foreshadows favorable developments for both Negro men and women.

FUTURE TRENDS: THE SCHOOLS

The second major line of development is education. Public interest in and concern with the quantity and quality of educational resources has quickened noticeably during the past few years. The American people are becoming aware that they should not permit the abilities of their children to be wasted, for the sake of the nation as well as for the sake of the children. To maintain the pace of its economic expansion and fulfill its commitments as a leader of the free world, the nation needs more well-trained men and women. It is difficult to see how this general stance of the American public could fail to help the Negro. The increase in the number of well-trained Negroes could be very great indeed. The single most underdeveloped human resource in the country is the Negro. If the nation is to fulfill its promise as a democracy it will have to do much more to develop the potential of its Negroes.

The American public's mounting concern with the adequacy of its educational effort was reflected in the President's recent message to the Congress on a bill to aid education. Among the principles the President advocated was that of making funds available to the states according to their need. Two thirds of the total Negro population live in the Southern states, which would receive a more than average share of Federal help under such a plan.[3]

It is too early to foretell, for the immediate future, the full consequences of the Supreme Court's decision on segregation in education. In some localities in the border states compliance with the new regulation has already taken place, and Negro children are now attending schools that are better equipped and better staffed. These Negro children will not grow up, as did their parents, cut off from normal relations with their white neighbors. In other localities, however, the Supreme Court's decision may result in at least a temporary deterioration in the schooling for both whites and Negroes. There is disturbing evidence that in several states certain white leaders are gaining support for plans that can only weaken the entire community and hamper the schooling of both white and Negro children.

The improvement of school buildings and teaching staffs and the integration of Southern schools are essential if Negroes are to have access to good educational preparation for life. But the extent to which Negroes benefit from future gains in these respects will depend in very large measure upon the extent to which Negro leaders and parents succeed in convincing the younger generation of the importance of working hard in school. To accomplish this many Negro families will have to reorder their lives and values. The schools can also help in this task, but only if they develop stronger teaching staffs and stronger guidance and counseling services. Rapid changes in the economic position of the Negro make it even more difficult for Negro than for white parents to provide guidance for their children about how best to prepare for life and work.

Leaders of the Negro community must guard against an

uncritical imitation of past approaches as more resources become available to improve the education of Negroes. For a long time, for example, Negro leaders in the South have justifiably complained about the limited amount and poor quality of vocational education available to Negroes. On the other hand, there is increasing evidence that sound knowledge of fundamental subjects is the best preparation for becoming a skilled worker. If a high school student has control over such basic subjects as mathematics, English, and science, industry finds it relatively easy to instruct him in specific skills. Moreover, these are the fundamentals required for admission to college. Although Negro leaders are right in pressing for broader and better vocational education both in the North and, particularly, in the South, it would be an error for them to place primary stress on this one aspect of secondary education.[4]

The cost of a higher education is a major obstacle for most Negroes. In recent years there have been sizable increases in scholarship aid, because of both state action and the activities of industry and other voluntary groups. To the extent that increases in scholarship aid take place it will be easier for a larger number of Negroes to attend college in the future than in the past.

Among the difficult problems confronting the Negro community is the future of many segregated colleges in the South. The weaknesses of many of these institutions show up very sharply when they are compared with the average college. As the Negro becomes more completely integrated into American industry and society, he needs more than ever before schooling equal to that of the white population. Among the recommendations that have been advanced is that many Negro colleges in the South should be transformed into technical institutes providing a strong two-year course of study. The technician occupations may well prove to be one of the most important areas of expanding employment opportunities in coming years. On the other hand, if some Negro colleges in the South are transformed into technical institutes, young Negroes in the South will be confronted with additional difficulties in securing a college degree because of the higher cost of going to an institution away from home.

In spite of many uncertainties, the general outlines of several important educational developments of the near future are relatively clear. The American people will invest more in education. To a considerable extent this larger investment will do no more than meet the increased costs of educating a rapidly growing student population. But some increase in educational expenditures per child will probably occur as the public comes to understand more fully the wastage now resulting from insufficient resources for developing the potential of many children, especially those of poor parents. Particular efforts will probably be made to develop a much larger part of the Negro potential. It is also probable that transformations within the Negro community will result in young Negroes being more strongly motivated to take advantage of the resources that are made available.

FUTURE TRENDS: THE FEDERAL GOVERNMENT

The third line of development relates to the Federal government, including the armed services. The effective integration of the Negro soldier during the last few years was summarized by the Department of Defense at the beginning of 1955 in a report which declared:

The Negro citizen in the Armed Forces is now utilized on the basis of individual merit and proficiency in meeting the needs of the Services.

Throughout the Army, Navy, Air Force, and Marine Corps, fully integrated units have replaced the all-Negro units which, until recent years, formed the only channel of military service for Negro enlistees and draftees since Colonial times.

Thorough evaluation of the battle-tested results to date indicates a marked increase in overall combat effectiveness through integration.

Economies in manpower, material, and money have resulted from the elimination of racially duplicated facilities and operations.

The program has advanced more rapidly than had been considered possible in some quarters, and there have been no untoward incidents.[5]

This is a remarkable story. But important problems remain. Integration is not yet fully accomplished in the Reserve Officers' Training Corps, or in the National Guard. Since the purpose of these civilian components is to offer maximum support to the armed forces in an emergency, it is essential that they be organized and trained along the lines of the armed forces' structure. This will be difficult to accomplish in the South since the National Guard units are instrumentalities of state governments as well as of the Federal government. Another problem within the military sphere is that opportunities for Negroes to obtain satisfactory civilian positions in the Department of Defense are still very limited. Although a few Negroes are employed in high level positions, the typical Negro civilian employee is a file clerk, clerk-typist, messenger boy, or cleaning woman.

The Department of Defense report also points out that integration in the armed forces extends far beyond the utilization of men in military assignments. "The Armed Forces, within their own sphere, have developed notable examples of racial coordination and integration in housing, transportation, religious worship, schooling, recreation, and other aspects of community life for service personnel and their families."[6] While several Southern states are defying the Supreme Court's school decision, the armed forces have integrated all schools on military installations. There is one exception where the problem is now being worked out in accordance with basic policy. Although it is easier to integrate a small number of Negro children in a post school than it is to integrate the public schools in a county where Negroes are a majority of the population, the success of the armed forces' challenge to tradition should help to convince many who are undecided that change is possible and advantageous to Negro and white alike.

Since the United States will continue to require sizable standing forces, a high proportion of the young men of the nation will continue to serve on active duty for two, three, or four years. This means that a large number of Southern whites and Negroes will have direct experience in living and working together as equals during a formative period of their lives. The armed services will continue to represent a pilot experiment in integration which will show that there is a practical alternative to segregation. Military service will provide a major dynamic force for remodeling race relations throughout the nation, particularly in the South.

In addition to its tremendous impact through the armed services, the Federal government will continue to exercise an important influence on the future position of the Negro. Consider the last fifteen years. Since the early days of World War II the Federal government has helped to overcome discriminatory employment practices. Recently, the government has taken energetic action to eliminate segre-

gation in the nation's capitol. In addition the government
has eliminated segregation of civilian personnel in its installations throughout the South. The Interstate Commerce
Commission has ordered the abandonment of separate seat-
ing and other discriminatory practices by common carriers
in interstate transportation. Particular mention must be
made of the Supreme Court, whose decisions are moving
in the direction of declaring unconstitutional all discriminatory practices based solely on race in all circumstances
where the Federal courts have jurisdiction.

For some time the Federal government has been seeking
to insure that employers with government contracts observe
antidiscriminatory policies. Many contractors in the South
are caught between Federal regulations and deep-seated
local antagonisms toward the Negro, frequently buttressed
by trade union practices and local ordinances. The Federal
government has been disinclined to resort to cancellation
or nonrenewal of contracts but is actively seeking the co-
operation of industry. President Eisenhower has stated:
"This problem and its solution are the job of all of us. Government can help and must help. But the final answer is
up to you and me and must be achieved in the communities where we live. Every American who opposes inequality, every American who helps, in even the smallest way,
to make equality of opportunity a living fact, is doing the
business of America. He is strength, against its enemies,
in the cause of freedom."[7]

An increasing number of Americans outside of the South
are willing to see the Federal government act energetically
to remove the barriers of discrimination as quickly as possible. In the years immediately ahead this attitude will
exercise a growing influence on Congressional action. This
means that any new Federal legislation, such as the impor-

tant aid for education bill, must be consistent with this approach. Congress will find it difficult, if not impossible, to pass new legislation that overtly or even tacitly reinforces existing segregation practices. Southern members of Congress may be able to defeat legislation favored by the majority of people, including even those living in the South, not on the virtues of specific proposals, but solely on grounds of their impact on segregation. Such action can lead to no more than useless conflict and delay. The trend of national policy has been clearly set.

The President of the United States is not only the head of the executive branch of the Federal government but the highest elected official in the country. As such he is the leader of the American people. President Eisenhower, as well as his two predecessors, Presidents Roosevelt and Truman, each made significant contributions to mobilizing public opinion against discriminatory barriers in the path of the Negro. There is every likelihood that future presidents of the United States will act in the same manner, out of both inner conviction and heightened awareness of the dangers to the international policy of the United States that unfair treatment of the Negro represents.

FUTURE TRENDS: THE COMMUNITY

The final major line of development relates to the role played by voluntary groups, particularly at the local level. Segregation cannot long survive unless it is supported by many individuals. Nor can it be abolished unless many individuals change their attitudes, feelings, and behavior. At the very least they must change their behavior. For generations the churches were a major bulwark of segregation in the South. The doctrines of Christianity were often used not to challenge the white population to behave

more justly and equitably towards Negroes but to justify
segregation and discrimination. Recently, however, the
Catholic Church and some of the Protestant groups have
taken aggressive action against segregation.

In recent years, the trade unions also have taken important measures against discrimination. At the national and
international level, union constitutions have been amended
by removing discriminatory clauses. Labor leaders have
spoken out strongly against unfair treatment of the Negro.
But segregation is often firmly entrenched at the local level.
Even in unions in which the national leadership has unequivocally declared for racial equality, many locals have
been able to maintain discriminatory practices. Gains have
been made, but, in general, and particularly in the South,
the gains to date have been small. The Negro cannot enjoy
a much greater degree of economic opportunity in the
South in the years immediately ahead unless local unions
change their practices. Such changes are most likely to
occur if other groups — government, industry, the church
— set an example. In such a situation it is difficult to con-
ceive of trade unions remaining far behind. Outside of the
South, it can be anticipated that the increasingly strong
commitment of the leaders of the unified American labor
movement to the eradication of racial discrimination will
prove an important lever in breaking down discriminatory
practices where they still exist.

Only community action can bring about desegregation
in housing. Southerners have frequently pointed out that
the North, too, practices segregation. Although Northern
communities do not regulate relations between the races by
law, segregation is firmly established in fact, as evidenced
by all-Negro neighborhoods and the resulting segregated

schools, segregated churches, segregated stores, and segregated recreational areas.

It would be foolish to minimize the difficulties of establishing integrated housing. But it is not necessary to exaggerate the difficulties. There are communities in the South where the housing of whites and Negroes has been less sharply segregated than in other areas of the country. In a few of the larger urban centers of the North integrated housing has been initiated in government financed projects. Although at first only a few white people may be willing to enter integrated projects, experience in some of them suggests that the problem can be resolved. Although it will be a long time before this major stronghold of segregation falls, more governmental and even private funds will probably become available for interracial housing projects in the near future.[8]

The major trends along each of the four lines of development which have been discussed all lead to the same general conclusion: the momentum established during the last decade and a half will result in accelerated improvement in the position of the Negro in the years immediately ahead. But there is one cloud on the horizon. The pressure exerted on the South by the Supreme Court to integrate its schools has sparked a countermovement dedicated to shoring up the entire system of segregation. It is difficult to estimate the strength of this countermovement. It is more than likely, however, that the forces that will continue to be exerted against discrimination from every side — government, the armed forces, industry, labor, science, religion — will induce the South to steer away from a self-destructive recalcitrance. Only if the South fails to see the inevitable outcome, only if it fails to add up the total cost of a doomed struggle, only then might it be so profligate as to waste its resources in fighting integration instead of using them constructively to solve the problem of relations between the races.

The greatest danger is that the enlightened moderate leadership of the South may permit extremists to take control. If the constructive forces in the South assume responsibility for directing the inevitable process of desegregation, they will cut the ground from under extremists in both North and South, and will provide a firm foundation for the development of the full potential of white and Negro alike.

LESSONS FOR MANPOWER POLICY

What lessons for manpower policy can be extracted from this review of the major factors that will determine how fully and how fast the Negro population will be able to develop its potential? The first lesson is a negative one. Until society places a higher value on the individual than it has done in the past, it will fail to take the constructive actions required to emancipate disadvantaged groups. Until a society recognizes the value of human potential, it will do little to develop it.

For several thousand years the religious tradition of the West has stressed the importance of the individual, but religion alone has often been unable to improve the social and economic status of individuals. Judaism and Christianity have helped in raising the level of social conscience, but religious conviction alone has seldom led men to relinquish special privilege voluntarily. Major gains have come when societies have recognized that the brawn and brains of all their citizens are required for the accomplishment of important goals. Dominant groups have been willing to give up their special privileges when they have seen the value of men as an economic or military resource.

Discrimination against one group by another is seldom based on a single consideration. The maintenance of a system of segregation is reinforced by the specific returns that the dominant group derives from the practice. Some of these are easy to recognize. Less apparent are the substantial costs that the dominant group pays for maintaining segregation. Those who take advantage of their fellow man pay a high price.

The elaboration of a system of rules to govern the relations between the dominant and the disadvantaged groups results in engulfing not only the minds but the emotions of all concerned. To challenge such a system is therefore difficult and frequently dangerous. A successful challenge hinges on four prior conditions: the development of effective leaders within the disadvantaged group; constructive leadership within the dominant group; a conducive environment which will help to cushion whatever changes are introduced; and time to learn about the new situation and adjust to it.

In order to abolish a system of discrimination, the disadvantaged group must have reached a level of self-development and of organization which permits its leadership to crystallize its legitimate demands. Unless these demands are put forward, the dominant group will let well enough alone. Significant alterations in established relations always involve serious stresses and strains. Some members of the dominant group are likely to lose income and power. Unless the proponents of change exert strong and persistent pressure, no significant changes are likely to take place.

But competent leadership in the disadvantaged group

is not enough to bring about the desired results, especially if the group is a minority. Help from outstanding individuals in the dominant group is also necessary. When such persons declare themselves, they act as a magnet and draw to the support of change others in the dominant group who are inclined to help. Moreover, their willingness to take a position helps to divide the opposition. Many individuals will favor the maintenance of the status quo only so long as they do not have to justify their position. Once they are challenged, they are likely to become neutrals if not actually protagonists of change. This leaves in outright opposition only those who insist upon their accustomed privileges without regard for the legitimate claims of other members of the society. To maintain the existing situation, recalcitrants must be willing to argue against the ethical and democratic principles accepted by the majority in the society. When the tide is turning fast, only a few are willing to stand against it.

Without men of ability and good will in both the disadvantaged and dominant groups, no significant changes are likely to take place. But successful introduction of change also depends in no small measure upon the environment. If the rights and privileges of the disadvantaged group can be increased without direct economic cost to members of the dominant group, acceptance of change will be eased. The history of the United States is testimony to the absorptive capacity of a nation that has been expanding most of the time. Tens of millions of European immigrants were quickly and successfully assimilated only because the economy offered a job to every man. A similarly conducive economic environment over the past fifteen years has given the Negro his opportunity.

To appreciate the importance of the economic factor all

that is required is to review the findings of Gunnar Myrdal's classic study of the American Negro, *An American Dilemma,* based upon conditions prevailing in the 1930's. His deep concern about the marginal status of the Negro in American society grew in large part out of his conclusion that the Negro had failed to gain a secure foothold in the industrial economy while his position in Southern agriculture was becoming weaker. The contrast between the conclusions emerging from Myrdal's study and those of this appraisal are one indication of how far the Negro has come within the last fifteen years.[9]

The most important element in effecting change is the element of time. The past cannot be expunged by a change of heart, for the evil that men do to each other leaves deep marks. It is an ironic tragedy that considerable time must pass before a disadvantaged group can make full use of new opportunities that have been made available to it. How much time depends on how deeply its ways of thinking, of feeling, of responding, have been affected by the disabilities it has suffered. The delay can be shortened both by help from its own leadership in adjusting to new conditions, and by continuing help from the leadership of the dominant group. But it behooves us all to remember that equality can never be bestowed — it can only be earned.

For hundreds of years the private conscience and the public morality of America have been weakened by the guilt we have carried over our treatment of the Negro. Ninety years ago we expended a great treasure to expiate this guilt. But with victory in our hands we let it out of our grasp. The North rushed into money-making and the South was busy binding up its wounds. The Negro was denied the new freedom that had been given him by the Constitution.

For generations we have continued to live with this guilt, doing a little from time to time to assuage our consciences. When called upon to help to free men from the forces of oppression in 1917, in 1941, and again in 1950, we did not falter. The greater challenge that now faces us as a leader of the free world has at last forced us to recall and to act upon Lincoln's warning: "Those who deny freedom to others deserve it not for themselves, and, under a just God, cannot long retain it."

NOTES

FOREWORD

[1] Eli Ginzberg and Douglas W. Bray, *The Uneducated* (New York, Columbia University Press, 1953).

[2] National Scholarship Service and Fund for Negro Students, *Interim Report—Southern Project, 1953-54 Activities,* Nov., 1954 (mimeographed).

[3] Eli Ginzberg, Sol W. Ginsburg, Sidney Axelrad, and John L. Herma, *Occupational Choice: An Approach to a General Theory* (New York, Columbia University Press, 1951).

[4] National Manpower Council, *A Policy for Skilled Manpower* (New York, Columbia University Press, 1954).

CHAPTER I

[1] This and other conferences held by the National Manpower Council on skilled workers are reported in *A Policy for Skilled Manpower.*

[2] See Douglas W. Bray, *Issues in the Study of Talent* (New York, King's Crown Press, 1954), Chap. II.

[3] See Ginzberg and Bray, *The Uneducated,* Chap. 2.

CHAPTER II

[1] The occupational progress of Negroes in recent years is analyzed in detail by John Hope II, "The Employment of Negroes in the United States by Major Occupation and Industry," in *The Relative Status of the Negro in the United States,* Yearbook Number, *The Journal of Negro Education,* XXII, No. 3, Summer, 1953, 307-21. See also U. S. Bureau of Labor Statistics, *Negroes in the United States: Their Employment and Economic Status,* Bulletin No. 1119 (Washington, D.C., Government Printing Office, Dec., 1952).

[2] U. S. Congress, Joint Committee on the Economic Report, *Characteristics of the Low-Income Population and Related Federal Programs* (Washington, D.C., Government Printing Office, 1955), p. 208.

[3] *Ibid.*, p. 213.

[4] *Development of Agriculture's Human Resources* (Washington, D.C., U. S. Department of Agriculture, 1955), pp. 25, 28.

[5] A. L. M. Wiggins, Board Chairman, Atlantic Coast Line Railroad, quoted in *U. S. News and World Report,* Jan. 27, 1956, p. 65.

[6] Lewis W. Jones, "The Negro Farmer," in *The Relative Status of the Negro in the United States,* p. 330. See also Lewis W. Jones, ed., *The Changing Status of the Negro in Southern Agriculture* (Rural Life Council, Tuskegee Institute, 1951).

[7] See Rupert B. Vance and Nicholas Demerath, eds., *The Urban South* (Chapel Hill, The University of North Carolina Press, 1954).

[8] The restricted employment opportunities of Negroes in Southern manufacturing are well documented in Donald Dewey, *Four Studies of Negro Employment in the Upper South* (Washington, D.C., National Planning Association, 1953).

[9] See The President's Committee on Government Contracts, *Second Annual Report* (Washington, D.C., Dec., 1955), pp. 8-9.

[10] Herman P. Miller, *Income of the American People* (New York, John Wiley & Sons, Inc., 1955), pp. 45-46, 65-68.

CHAPTER III

[1] See *A Policy for Skilled Manpower,* Chap. III.

[2] Ginzberg and Bray, *The Uneducated,* Chapters 3, 9, 12.

[3] A recent comprehensive treatment of Negro education is Harry S. Ashmore, *The Negro and the Schools* (Chapel Hill, The University of North Carolina Press, 1954). See also Ernst W. Swanson and John A. Griffin, eds., *Public Education in the South Today and Tomorrow: A Statistical Survey* (Chapel Hill, The Univerty of North Carolina Press, 1955).

[4] These estimates are based on Census data showing the number of years of school completed by men in various young

age groups in 1950. Substantial educational gains in the years preceding 1950 are not fully reflected in the estimates because most of those within each age group completed their schooling a number of years before 1950. Consequently all figures in Tables 13 and 14 are low. There are no data showing the actual annual number of Negro high school graduates outside the South, or the annual number of Negro college graduates. U. S. Office of Education data show that the number of Negro males who graduated from segregated Southern high schools increased from 9,768 in the academic year 1945-46 to 17,917 in 1949-50.

[5] See footnote 4. The reader may derive estimates for women alone by subtracting the figures in Table 13 from the corresponding figures in Table 14. The actual number of Negro females who graduated from segregated Southern high schools increased from 21,561 in 1945-46 to 26,052 in 1949-50.

[6] Quoted by Joseph W. Holley, *Education and the Segregation Issue* (New York, The William Frederick Press, 1955), p. 15.

[7] National Manpower Council, *A Policy for Scientific and Professional Manpower* (New York, Columbia University Press, 1953), p. 85.

[8] *Interim Report,* pp. 12-17. See also the Fund's *Southern Project Report, 1953-55* (March, 1956) for a general treatment of the problems involved in seeking to increase the number of Negroes who receive a good higher education.

[9] Harold A. Ferguson and Richard L. Plaut, "Talent—To Develop or Lose," *The Educational Record,* April, 1954, p. 137-40.

[10] Arthur L. Benson, "Problems of Evaluating Test Scores of White and Negro Teachers," Southern Association of Colleges and Secondary Schools, *Proceedings of the Fifty-ninth Annual Meeting* (1954), pp. 168-76.

CHAPTER IV

[1] See Dennis D. Nelson, *The Integration of the Negro into the U. S. Navy* (New York, Farrar, Straus and Young, 1951).

[2] For further material on the history of the Negro soldier in the United States, see Lee Nichols, *Breakthrough on the Color Front* (New York, Random House, 1954).

³ Most of the statistical material in this chapter is based on unpublished data generously prepared for the Conservation of Human Resources Project by the Department of the Army, particularly the Adjutant General's Office and the Surgeon General's Office, and by the Selective Service System.

⁴ Samuel A. Stouffer, *et al.*, *Studies in Social Psychology in World War II*, Vol. I: *The American Soldier: Adjustment During Army Life* (Princeton, Princeton University Press, 1949), p. 492.

⁵ A detailed evaluation of the performance of poorly educated soldiers in World War II, and of the Army's problems in utilizing them, is contained in Ginzberg and Bray, *The Uneducated.*

⁶ See also Robert R. Palmer, Bell I. Wiley, and William R. Keast, *The Procurement and Training of Ground Combat Forces* (Washington, D.C., Historical Division, Department of the Army, 1948), pp. 53-58.

⁷ U.S. Senate, Committee on Military Affairs, *Hearings on a Bill to Amend the Selective Training and Service Act of 1940, Oct. 14 and 15, 1942* (Washington, D.C., Government Printing Office, 1942), pp. 31-32.

⁸ Mark W. Clark, *Calculated Risk* (New York, Harper and Brothers, 1950), p. 414.

⁹ Stouffer, *The American Soldier,* pp. 588-90.

¹⁰ For a review of psychiatric screening of registrants and service men during World War II, see Eli Ginzberg, John L. Herma, and Sol W. Ginsburg, *Psychiatry and Military Manpower Policy* (New York, King's Crown Press, 1953).

¹¹ See especially Chap. 4.

¹² The Southeast is here defined to consist of: Alabama, Arkansas, Florida, Georgia, Kentucky, Louisiana, Mississippi, North Carolina, South Carolina, Tennessee, Virginia, and Washington, D.C.

¹³ See Stouffer, *The American Soldier,* pp. 545-49.

¹⁴ The effects of segregation on performance are discussed in *Freedom to Serve,* a report by the President's Committee on Equality of Treatment and Opportunity in the Armed Services (Washington, D.C., Government Printing Office, 1950).

¹⁵ Only one out of six of all Negroes in the theater were in

the upper three groups. Stouffer, *The American Soldier*, p. 588.

[16] See the following: Nichols, *Breakthrough on the Color Front*. James C. Evans and David A. Lane, Jr., "Integration in the Armed Services," in *Racial Desegregation and Integration, The Annals of the American Academy of Political and Social Science*, March, 1956, pp. 78-85. Reactions to the beginnings of integration within the European command are also reviewed in a memorandum prepared by Eli Ginzberg for the Historical Division of the Army in Europe, dated Oct. 26, 1955.

CHAPTER V

[1] *A Policy for Skilled Manpower*, p. 127.

[2] See Ginzberg and associates, *Occupational Choice*, for an analysis of the ways in which the early development of the child affects his later attitudes towards work.

[3] E. Franklin Frazier, "Problems and Needs of Negro Children and Youth," in *The Negro Child and Youth in the American Social Order*, Yearbook Number, *The Journal of Negro Education*, XIX, No. 3, Summer, 1950, 269-77.

[4] The relationship between occupational goals and school motivation is considered in Bray, *Issues in the Study of Talent*, Chap. IV.

[5] P. 131.

[6] The limitations of vocational education available for Negro students are spelled out more fully in *A Policy for Skilled Manpower*, pp. 191-92.

CHAPTER VI

[1] U.S. Congress, Joint Committee on the Economic Report, *A Program for the Low-Income Population at Substandard Levels of Living* (Washington, D.C., Government Printing Office, 1956), pp. 10-11.

[2] For a discussion of the probable effects of automation on the demand for labor, see George B. Baldwin, "Automation and the Skills of the Labor Force," in the National Manpower Council's *Improving the Work Skills of the Nation* (New York, Columbia University Press, 1955), pp. 83-98.

[3] The President's message, delivered on Jan. 12, 1956, was reprinted in the New York *Times,* Jan. 13, 1956, p. 12.

[4] A discussion of the limited vocational education facilities available to Negroes in a Northern state is found in *Training of Negroes in the Skilled Trades* (Hartford, Connecticut Commission on Civil Rights, 1954).

[5] Office of the Assistant Secretary of Defense (Manpower and Personnel), *Integration in the Armed Services: A Progress Report* (Washington, D.C., Jan., 1955), p. 9.

[6] *Ibid.,* p. 9.

[7] From a statement made on Oct. 9, 1952, quoted in the Foreword to *Equal Job Opportunity Is Good Business* (Washington, D.C., The President's Committee on Government Contracts, 1954). See also the Committee's *Second Annual Report.*

[8] See Robert C. Weaver, "Integration in Public and Private Housing," *Annals of the American Academy,* March, 1956, pp. 86-97.

[9] Gunnar Myrdal, *An American Dilemma: The Negro Problem and Modern Democracy* (New York, Harper and Brothers, 2 vols., 1944).